T0127671

Tan Siak Kew

Going Against the Grain

Tan Siak Kew

Going Against the Grain

Fiona Tan

With Foreword by
S R Nathan

 **World Scientific**

NEW JERSEY · LONDON · SINGAPORE · BEIJING · SHANGHAI · HONG KONG · TAIPEI · CHENNAI

Published by

World Scientific Publishing Co. Pte. Ltd.
5 Toh Tuck Link, Singapore 596224
USA office: 27 Warren Street, Suite 401-402, Hackensack, NJ 07601
UK office: 57 Shelton Street, Covent Garden, London WC2H 9HE

Library of Congress Cataloging-in-Publication Data
Tan, Fiona (Independent writer) author.
  Tan Siak Kew : going against the grain / Fiona Tan (independent writer).
  pages cm
  ISBN 978-9814603072 (hardcover : alk. paper) -- ISBN 978-9814623605 (softcover : alk. paper)
  1. Tan, Siak Kew, 1903–1977. 2. Teochew (Chinese people)--Singapore--Biography.
3. Businessmen--Singapore--Biography. 4. Singapore--History--20th century. I. Title. II. Title:
Going against the grain.
  DS610.63.T36T36 2014
  305.895'105957092--dc23
  [B]
                                                                2014024075

British Library Cataloguing-in-Publication Data
A catalogue record for this book is available from the British Library.

In-house Editors: Chye Shu Wen/Rajni Gamage

Typeset by Stallion Press
Email: enquiries@stallionpress.com

Printed in Singapore

"For many historians, the period from the late colonial days to our early years of independence was an exciting time of political contestation and activism. This book introduces us to a Singaporean who played a central role in important institutions during this period of ferment, holding a variety of high positions, but whose story has been largely untold. One reason could be that he did not attract the fame or notoriety of controversy and his speeches reproduced in this book reflect a man with a firm but even-handed tone. From a professional perspective, I was delighted to see that some speeches highlighted are from the invaluable records of the Singapore Chinese Chamber of Commerce that are currently under the preservation care of the National Archives of Singapore. Photographs, oral history, and newspapers discovered in the archives and collections of our National Archives and National Library also enrich the book that is now in your hands. Archives play a multitude of roles — from the administrative to the legal to its cultural and historical objectives — but archives also help our society to recall its stories. Archival practice has come to embrace the fact that records from social and organisational activity leave "traces" that can bring a biography to life and to show us links and relationships to people, places, and events we are familiar with. As Singapore approaches its golden jubilee and remembers our pioneers, this book will add to our memories of Singaporeans who made a difference."

Eric Chin
Director, National Archives of Singapore

Foreword

It was sometime around late 1966 that I first met the late Ambassador Tan Siak Kew. I was then a junior official in the Foreign Ministry of Singapore. I was a little apprehensive about meeting such a well-known member of the Chinese business community. After greeting him and exchanging a few words, he immediately put me at ease by his gentle scholarly demeanour.

In due time, I came to know more about him. Thus, I developed a respectful relationship that grew with time. When he was appointed Singapore's first Ambassador to the Kingdom of Thailand, I had more occasions to interact with him, both in the course of official duties and social functions. They took place both in the Foreign Ministry in Singapore as well as in Bangkok. I was enriched by his humble ways, from his charming anecdotes from his life. After these conversations, new thoughts about the nature of things and life's uncertainties came to me vividly. I found myself seeking to know more at the end of each such conversation with him. I found a quietly humane person behind that stern face.

This book brings to light the details of his experiences in life. It is a story of one of our fellow Singaporeans, of our founding generation, whose life has been summed up in the following terms — "A scholar by inclination, a businessman by necessity, and a diplomat by duty". A reading of *Going Against the Grain* will reveal much about this versatile Singaporean, who rose from humble beginnings to eminence in Singapore's society. That story should inspire both young and old, and show what Singapore offers by way of opportunities for one who is willing to strive and succeed.

The late Tan Siak Kew's public life was indeed a case of going against the grain. Looking back on his unusual and varied road to success, his story indeed defies stereotypes. He came from China and made Singapore his home. He enriched himself by seeking education, both in English and Chinese. He flourished in business and emerged as a leader of the Teochew community by first rising to prominence in the Singapore Chinese Chamber of Commerce, and eventually emerging as its President in 1965. In colonial times, his leadership within civil society was recognised, leading to him being made Nominated Member of the Colonial Legislative Assembly in 1958–1959. All his life, he strove hard to be a bridge between Singapore's English-speaking and other Chinese-speaking communities in various educational endeavours. When Singapore was granted independence, he widened that mission to other local communities. As Ambassador to Thailand — the first from independent Singapore — he excelled using his extensive business contacts and links with the Thai Establishment to promote Singapore in Thailand. I was privileged to know this father-figure of a man and learn much from him.

S. R. Nathan
Former President of Singapore

A Word From ...

"I got to know the late Tan Siak Kew when I started working in Kheng Leong, my family's commodity firm, in the early 1950s. His company, Buan Lee Seng, was also in the commodity business run by his eldest son, Puay Yong. I used to play tennis with Puay Yong in their residence in Scotts Road. When I started to work at United Overseas Bank, the late Tan Siak Kew was Chairman of Sze Hai Tong Bank (or Four Seas Communications Bank). He was always ready with good advice for me. He was an honest and straightforward person and a shrewd businessman well respected in the business community and banking fraternity."

Wee Cho Yaw
Chairman Emeritus & Adviser of United Overseas Bank

"I came to know Tan Siak Kew during my days as a journalist in Sin Chew Jit Poh and Nanyang Siang Pau. He was always very sober and careful with his statements. When I was in charge of Chinese education as Parliamentary Secretary of Ministry of Education in 1962, the Nanyang University hit a snag with the government when the police were about to be sent to the university to arrest students. I advised then Prime Minister Lee Kuan Yew not to do that and he handed the problem of Nantah to me. I called up Ko Teck Kin and Tan Siak Kew to my office to discuss how to settle the Nantah problem. I asked them what they really wanted and Tan Siak Kew said: "We want to ensure that the government continues to acknowledge Chinese as a medium of instruction and that there will not be any changes." I phoned up the Prime Minister to ask his views and he accepted the proposal. This temporarily settled the Nantah problem. Under Tan Siak Kew's leadership, Nantah reformed along the lines as required by the government. Unfortunately, his dream did not come through because Nantah was later merged with the University of Singapore to form the National University of Singapore in 1980. I was not consulted when this decision was made. Tan Siak Kew devoted a lot of his time promoting Chinese education and better understanding between the English- and Chinese-educated communities. He was indeed a rare businessman who spent so much time, energy, and money in upgrading our society. He contributed a great deal to the nation and remains a good example for younger businessmen to follow."

Lee Khoon Choy
Former Senior Minister of State & Ambassador of Singapore

Contents

Introduction

China, 1920. Picture a young Tan Siak Kew, sitting by the river in Teo Ann, watching ships sail north. He quietly sheds a tear, as he realises that unlike his peers aboard those ships waving to their families and friends, he would not be able to afford to go to the institutes of higher learning in Beijing or Shanghai.[1]

Siak Kew never attended university in northern China, or anywhere for that matter. Instead, he sailed south — very far south indeed — to Malaya and Singapore, where he gradually and successfully made a name for himself, as a trader, a community leader, a nominated legislative Assemblyman, a non-career diplomat, a philanthropist, and an avid supporter of education.

A reporter in 1966 described Siak Kew as 'a scholar by inclination, a businessman by necessity, a diplomat by duty.'[2] This apt description encompassed the multi-varied nature of Siak Kew's public life, who not only possessed a keen scholastic mind with a talent for languages and business but also was a fervent supporter of education, President of the Chinese Chamber of Commerce for multiple terms, Singapore's first Ambassador to Thailand, nominated

Figure 1.   A photo of a young Siak Kew, in the Seventh Anniversary publication of the Singapore Chinese Mandarin School, published in 1937. Siak Kew was one of the editors for this publication.
Source: *Singapore Mandarin School Seventh Anniversary Publication* (Singapore: Overseas Chinese Mandarin School, 1937). [新加坡华侨国语学校第七周年纪念特刊 (新加坡: 华侨国语学校, 1937)].

member of the Legislative Assembly, community leader of the Teochew community, and notable philanthropist of his time.

Despite his prolific contributions, there has not been any publication dedicated to this remarkable man. This is, however, not an exhaustive biography for several reasons — chief among them being that the man himself is no longer around to fill in the gaps left behind by the records. Another compounding difficulty was Siak Kew's personality — a humble and unassuming figure who avoided the public eye and thus left little of his thoughts on record.

Instead, one must rely on newspaper articles, meeting minutes, commemorative write-ups, and memories as recounted by his acquaintances and family, to reconstruct his life. All secondary accounts have their inherent limitations. Even when supplemented by interviews with his son and people who knew him, it is implausible that any biography, composed posthumously, can capture Siak Kew's innermost thoughts and the motivations behind his actions. However, these are risks that must be taken, and even if unresolved, an attempt must be made at presenting these conflicting representations of Siak Kew's life, before these gaps become wider and memories become forever lost.

Given these restrictions and considerations, this is less a biography than a collection of vignettes of a pioneer all but forgotten, who in his understated and quiet manner, did his best to contribute to Singapore's development. Nevertheless, these various flashpoints of his life are strung together in a more or less chronological fashion, and arranged in thematic chapters. The first chapter is a sketchy outline of his family and life, insofar as they had an effect on his public life. The next covers the lead up to the Japanese Occupation, which was a defining ordeal for both Singapore and Siak Kew. The subsequent chapters are less chronological and more thematic, a reflection of the many different hats he wore in post-war Singapore. The chapters cover many aspects of his public life, such as his efforts to fight for citizenship rights in Singapore, his business philosophy and role in the Singapore Chinese Chamber, his regional role in establishing both trade and diplomatic links, and his contributions to the Nantah experiment.

As this mammoth excavation project progressed, it was rewarding to realise that the results of the metaphorical digging went beyond an abstract filling of historical gaps. It was interesting to speak to interviewees and realise that these primary source records salvaged from the murky waters of history jolted certain memories.

While reading a comment by Yap Pheng Geck describing how he was imprisoned together with Ching Kee San and Siak Kew, Tan Puay Hiang, Siak Kew's youngest son, suddenly recalled how Siak Kew used to bring him to Ching's mansion when he was younger. Now he understood why his father had such ties with Ching; it was the result of the common hardship they had been through during the war. Such was an example of an instance where the historical record contextualised memories. These chance finds showed how historical research need not always be impersonal and could in fact have a tangible impact on the individual.

While this humble publication does not attempt to be the definitive text on this pioneer in Singapore's recent history, it nevertheless will be of interest not only to people who are interested in Siak Kew's life and times, but also members of the public who wish to learn about the unchartered roads in Singapore's history. This is the story of both Siak Kew and the history of Singapore as it transitioned towards nationhood. While Singapore's history could be traced back 700 years, this begins with a more conventional beginning at Siak Kew's birth in Teo Ann in 1903.

Birth of a Character

以君年少英俊学富力强，且积极熟土产学，将来进展，无限量也。
尤热心公益事业，输资不少，亦南洋之慈善家也。

He is a young and educated man, and is passionate about learning
more about local produce. His future development is limitless. He is
also passionate about philanthropy, and has contributed a lot to
charity, and can be counted among Nanyang's notable philanthropists.

— *Biographer Song Lusheng's comment on Tan Siak Kew in 1934* [i]

---

[i] Found in Song Lusheng, *Far-East Biographies* (Singapore: Centre for Far East Biographies,
1934) [宋鲁生, *远东人物志* (新加坡 : 远东民史纂修所, 1934)].

Tan Siak Kew was born on 31 May 1903[3], in Kim Sar (金砂寨), a county in Teo Ann (潮安) district, in Guangdong (广东) Province. Like many of the Chinese immigrants in Singapore, Siak Kew hailed from Southern China. His family, however, was no stranger to Nanyang, a term loosely translated as the Southern Seas, and used by Chinese communities to describe Malaya, Singapore, and the Dutch East Indies.[ii]

Figure 2.   Family home of Siak Kew in Kim Sar.
Source: Image courtesy of Mr Tan Puay Hiang during visit in 2013.

[ii]Author's note: This chapter on Siak Kew's early personal life is largely based on discussions with his son, Tan Puay Hiang, as well as Chinese biographies of notable Chinese of the period: namely the 1934 and 1941 editions of *Far-East Biographies* (Penang: Centre for Far East Biographies) [远东人物志 (槟城：远东民史纂修所)] and Song Zhemei (ed.), *Biographies of Singapore-Malaya Personalities* (Hong Kong: Southeast Asia Research Institute, 1969) [宋哲美 (ed.), 星马人物志 (香港：东南亚研究所, 1969)]. Much of it is shrouded in mystery and might perhaps be considered hearsay by historians of the empiricist persuasion, especially when they contradict each other. Nevertheless, in the absence of alternatives and with a note of caution, they are used in this chapter to attempt a reconstruction of the man's early life.

Figure 3. Siak Kew is second from right in this photograph of the family at a relative's funeral in 1926.
Source: Image courtesy of Mr Tan Puay Hiang.

Trading Roots

Siak Kew's grandfather was a successful cotton and cotton yarn trader with business networks spanning Swatow, Hong Kong, and Shanghai. One could say trading runs in the family, although Siak Kew's father, Tan Jiaxiang (陈家祥)[iii], was more inclined towards calligraphy. In the 1880s, Siak Kew's eldest uncle ventured to the Southern Seas to set up pepper and gambier plantations in Malaya. He also joined many other Teochews in developing pepper and date plantations in Johor.

[iii] Author's note on romanisation of names: Where more common forms of phonetic romanisation is available for the Chinese terms, they are used instead of the modern Hanyu Pinyin. For instance, 潮州八邑会管 is romanised as Teochew Poit Ipp Huay Kuan, instead of the uncommon and potentially misleading Chaozhou Bayi Huiguan.

Nicknamed Little Swatow (小汕头), Johor Bahru had historically a significant Teochew presence. Economic histories on the development of pepper and gambier plantations in Johor, as well as local histories on the social role played by extended brotherhood organisations such as Ngee Heng Kongsi in Johor all elaborate on the important roles played by the predominantly Teochew Chinese population in Johor.[4] Siak Kew's eldest uncle was one of the many Teochews involved in this.

When his eldest uncle passed away, Siak Kew's father and fourth uncle took over the business. Not much is known about the scale of the business, save that the trading firm, Tai Lai Hang (泰来行), dealing mainly with pepper and gambier, was based in Singapore by the early twentieth century.

Settling Down in Singapore

In 1910, seven-year-old Siak Kew and his two brothers accompanied their mother on a long voyage across the South China Sea to join their father in Singapore. Siak Kew was enrolled into St Anthony's Boys' School, along Victoria Street. Established and run by a Catholic Portugese Mission since 1893, St Anthony's Boys' School gave Siak Kew the advantage his Chinese-educated father did not have — an English-language education.

Siak Kew's academic prowess was clear to all when he had a double promotion, performing so well at a joint examination for Third and Fourth Standards that he was allowed to skip Standard Three. And it was no fluke, as he had three such double promotions during his school career.[5] He scored well enough to enter Raffles Institution, though he left without graduating at age 15 to accompany his aged father back to China. It was during the two years in China, that Siak Kew began to lament his lack of a Chinese education.

He enrolled in a private school which offered traditional Chinese education in his hometown, and began learning the classics.

He returned to Singapore in 1921, and stayed with his eldest brother, Tan Siak Kuang, who was in his late twenties and working at the Oversea-Chinese Bank. Embarrassed at being reliant on his brother, the young Siak Kew sought employment at the Overseas Assurance Corporation (华侨保险公司). This was a prominent local firm offering fire, marine, and motor car insurance, with a Board of Directors which read like a who's who list of prominent Chinese businessmen, including Lim Nee Soon, S.Q. Wong, Ong Boon Tat, and Lim Kim Seng.

Reluctant to cease learning, Siak Kew would travel from Chulia Street to Beach Road for night classes in business at Raffles Institution. While he understood the edge that an English-language education would give him in a British colony, Siak Kew also wanted to ensure that he did not neglect his cultural heritage as a Chinese. Thus, he also continued his Chinese education with the assistance of a private tutor at home and through enrollment in the Singapore Chinese Mandarin School (新加坡华侨国语学校), located at Prinsep Street. Through sheer determination and tireless learning, Siak Kew became bilingual, a trait that would come in useful when he rose to become a business community leader.

In fact, his Chinese was so impressive that he was the editor of the Seventh Anniversary publication of the Singapore Chinese Mandarin School, which promoted the study of Mandarin. He was aware of the challenges faced by the promotion of the study of Mandarin, hence his calligraphic foreword to the publication ended not with a self-congratulatory refrain, but an exhortation to continue striving (乃须努力).[6]

His introduction also contained an eloquent and humble explanation of the reasons why. This self-effacing, humble spirit always spurred Siak Kew to strive for further greatness. Reflected in this

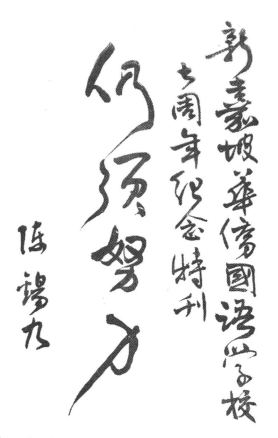

Figure 4. Calligraphic foreword contributed by Siak Kew, emphasising the need for the school to continue striving.

Source: *Singapore Mandarin School Seventh Anniversary Publication* (Singapore: Overseas Chinese Mandarin School, 1937) [新加坡华侨国语学校第七周年纪念特刊 (新加坡: 华侨国语学校, 1937)].

introduction he penned in 1937, it is not difficult to imagine that this character of his had been present even as a young boy in St Anthony's, or a youthful lad in the Overseas Assurance Corporation.

Extending Roots

In 1924, Siak Kew married Leow Moey Cheng, fifth daughter of Leow Chia Heng (廖正兴). Leow (1874–1934) was a prominent

編　者　語

陳錫九

本校是次發行七週年紀念特刊，蓋有三大目的與兩大希望存焉。目的者何？七年以來本校設施之概況，以及學者對於研究國語之興趣，得以報告關心於本校之人士，一也。借重文字之力量，聯絡同學之情感，人手一卷，學校之光榮如在目前，二也。華社曾顧言關於提倡國語之弘業，為團結作擴大之宣傳，集同學之作品，以觀學習國語之成效，三也。希望者何？本校同學研究國語為時未久，初學之人，莫知其要，自信之能力薄弱，編輯特刊，述其所已知，及其所未知，希望社會人士與以有力之指導，冀抛磚引玉之效，此其一也。近來僑生為潮流所鼓動，欲習國語者日眾，但以對於中國文字，毫無根柢，將進越退，未敢造次，茲特刊物，同學寫其過去學習國語之艱辛，及其進步之程度，於以見學習國語之容易，鼓勵僑生向學之決心，此又其一也。為此三大目的，與兩大希望，用敢不揣譾陋，毅然印行，區區之忱，尚祈熱心教育人士，加以指導為幸。

二　　　　　　　　　　　　　　　　　　七週年特刊

Figure 5.　Translation: This publication is to commemorate the school's seventh anniversary, with three goals in mind and two wishes to fulfil. What are its goals? Firstly, it has been seven years since the establishment of the school and it is time to update those interested in the study of Mandarin and to update those concerned about our school. Secondly, this is a chance to borrow the power of words, to connect the emotions of our students, to collectively explain the prospects of the school. Thirdly, it is to promote the study of Mandarin through the works of our students. What are its hopes? We are but a young school, and our students have not been studying Mandarin for a long time. We know our limitations and can only discuss what we know, but not what we have yet to know. Hence, we hope society can continue to support us, and maybe through our efforts, we can draw in further experts. Many overseas-born Chinese are now excited about learning Mandarin, but have nowhere to go. We hope this publication will encourage them to take it up, once they understand how easy it is. Thus are our three goals and two hopes. We hope passionate educators will be willing to overlook our shortcomings and continue to guide and support us.

Source: *Singapore Mandarin School Seventh Anniversary Publication* (Singapore: Overseas Chinese Mandarin School, 1937) [新加坡华侨国语学校第七周年纪念特刊 (新加坡: 华侨国语学校, 1937)].

Tan Siak Kew: Going Against the Grain　11

Teochew businessman who hailed from Teo Ann as well. Dabbling in produce trade, plantations, and even banking, Leow was one of the founders of the Chinese Chamber of Commerce in 1905 and the founder of Sze Hai Tong Bank, founded in 1906 to provide financial services to Chinese businessmen who felt slighted by British banks. Like many Chinese business leaders of the time, he was also a philanthropist, contributing to the establishment of the Tuan Mong School, one of the founding members of the Teochew Poit Ipp Huay Kuan (潮州八邑会管), a district-based community organisation that catered to eight provinces in Teochew, and also a founder of the Ngee Ann Kongsi.

The marriage might have seemed puzzling to some biographers, who could not resist penning a few lines to explain the reasons behind the marriage, as if trying to answer why a Teochew business leader of his time would allow his daughter to marry a clerk, albeit a hardworking and well-educated one. Song Lusheng, writing in 1934, attributed this union to Siak Kew's strong work ethic at the insurance company, which earned him the recognition of his peers and superiors.[7] Song Zhemei, writing much later in 1969, suggested that Siak Kew's late father had been friends with Leow, and that this marriage was match-made by family friends.[8] With both parties now deceased, it seems futile to try to reconstruct this rather trivial aspect of Siak Kew's life.

The answer is probably rather simple and innocuous. The Chinese business community was one that was divided very much upon dialect lines during the colonial period and social mobility was rather fluid. Given that Siak Kew was working in a reputable firm, and a fellow Teochew, it is understandable that Leow felt he would make a good addition to the family.

For Siak Kew, this marriage was a fruitful one on both the personal and professional fronts, giving him two sons and a daughter, and offering him an official introduction to trading. With his father-in-law's encouragement, he left the Overseas Assurance Corporation and joined Buan Mui Seng (万美成公司) as a manager, together with his brothers-in-law. For eight years, Siak Kew picked up the ropes of trading pepper and gambier.

In 1931, a personal setback struck as his wife, Moey Cheng died suddenly. Burdened with the sudden loss and the grave responsibility of caring for three young children, Siak Kew needed to clear his mind. He withdrew his shares from Buan Mui Seng and returned to China for several months. Touring the Zhejiang region, the sharp business acumen in him could not help but notice business opportunities. He returned to Singapore reinvigorated and ready to strike out on his own, reluctant to remain in the shadows of his late father-in-law. Together with two friends, he set up Buan Lee Seng (154–156 Boat Quay), which engaged in the trade of pepper and other local produce.

Siak Kew later remarried to Yeo Choon Siang (杨春仙), third daughter of Yeo Jizhao (杨吉兆). Yeo was a plantation owner who was also a staunch nationalist. In fact, he was one of the six philanthropists who bought Wan Qing Yuan (晚晴园) in 1937 and preserved it as a historical site.[9] The villa, located along Balestier Road, had been a place where noted revolutionary Sun Yat-Sen had stayed prior to 1911, and is today known as the Sun Yat-Sen Memorial Hall. His marriage to Choon Siang was a long and happy one, adding four sons and two daughters to the family.

By the end of the 1930s, Siak Kew had established himself as a leading trader of pepper and gambier. In 1937, he took on a leadership role in the business community as a committee member of the Singapore Chinese Chamber of Commerce, representing the interests of Teochew businessmen. Through a combination of his relentless hard work and his networks, Siak Kew was able to build a reputation for himself. Through his two marriages, Siak Kew not only gained business expertise and valuable contacts, but more importantly, was inspired to serve the community through philanthropy.

Figure 6.   Wan Qing Yuan on Tai Gin Road, 1970.
Source: Straits Times © Singapore Press Holdings Ltd. Reprinted with permission.

Red Sun over Malaya

When the Japanese landed in Singapore in 1942, all those in the China
Relief Fund were imprisoned by the Kempeitai. He was taken in for
three weeks and his family almost gave up hope. Then he was released
but simply lived quietly with his wife and [eight] children.[iv] During the
war, his business was lost.

— *Mr Tan Puay Hiang, youngest son of Tan Siak Kew, recounting what*
happened to his father during the Japanese Occupation[v]

[iv] Author's note: One of his sons passed away in the 1930s as a young child.
[v] Cited from Melanie Chew, *Leaders of Singapore* (Singapore: Resource Press, 1996), p. 43.

T he 1930s was an eventful period for Siak Kew, with the demise of his first wife and starting his own trading business. The developments abroad and locally, with the encroachment of Japanese expansionists in China, and the effects it had on the overseas Chinese community in Singapore, also began to push Siak Kew towards public service. Siak Kew began assuming the role of a community leader, both in the eyes of the Chinese community and the British colonial officials.

Looming Clouds

Siak Kew had been no stranger to philanthropy and helping those in need. Way back in 1920, he had donated $5 to the China Relief Fund, by no means an insignificant sum considering his clerical salary then.[10] Even when it did not particularly impact the communities he felt most attached to, Siak Kew also helped, such as his donation of $5 to the Salvation Army's call for donations to maintain the homes in Malaya in 1937.[11] While it might appear to be a small sum, it is pertinent to compare his personal contribution to an organisation such as Sze Hai Tong Bank, which had a much deeper pocket but only donated $10. Seen in this light, Siak Kew's $5 donation to this rather Eurocentric organisation is remarkable.[12] Needless to say, Siak Kew was far more generous with his own community, when he served in a fund-raising committee formed by the Chinese Chamber of Commerce, and took a personal lead in donating $500 to the Szechuan Relief Fund, set up to aid the hundreds of thousands of Chinese who were starving due to a drought that ruined the harvest of 1937.[13]

While Siak Kew had never publicly expressed any strong political views, his philanthropic streak led him into overseas Chinese nationalism. Political events in China had a trickle-down effect on the Chinese community in Malaya, especially the China-born Chinese such as Siak Kew and his peers in the Chamber of Commerce. As early as 1919, the effects of anti-Japanese sentiments over the unfair Treaty of Versailles had seeped into Singapore, culminating in protests in Kreta Ayer. The 1930s saw more of these sporadic political actions in Malaya due to Japanese expansionism in China, when the Japanese took over Manchuria in September 1931, and the battle in Shanghai in January 1932. In both cases, the Chinese Chamber of Commerce held meetings and passed resolutions to encourage the colonial government to censure Japan in the League of Nations, which Japan unilaterally withdrew from in 1933.[14] Perhaps it was due to the trials and tribulations he was dealing with in his personal life during this period, or his predominantly English-language education which did not endear him to the actions taken by the overtly nationalistic Chinese-educated,[15] but it was not until the Marco Polo Bridge Incident on 7 July 1937 that Siak Kew found himself drawn into the folds of the overseas Chinese nationalism.

Following the Marco Polo Bridge Incident, which was the first major battle between Chinese and Japanese troops in Shanghai in August, a mass meeting was called by Tan Kah Kee (陈嘉庚) at the Singapore Chinese Chamber of Commerce on 15 August, two days after the battle in Shanghai began. The Chinese Chamber was packed with representatives from 119 institutions, including Chinese schools, clubs, guilds, and associations. A five-minute-per-representative rule had to be imposed to ensure an orderly meeting, amidst shouts of 'Long Live the Republican Government of China'. At this spirited meeting, Siak Kew was appointed as one of the Teochew representatives in the fund-raising committee, which consisted of thirty-one prominent Chinese businessmen.[16] This was probably his initiation into taking the lead in large-scale philanthropy.

Within days, $250,000 was raised. Donations poured in from a broad spectrum of the overseas Chinese community in Singapore, from *towkays* to small shopkeepers to cabaret girls, all contributing what they could. Even those who could not afford monetary donations helped out in other ways. For instance, students sold confectionery to raise funds, and those in the entertainment industry, such as songstresses and actresses, held benefit events to raise funds. As one of the nine Teochew representatives of the Singapore Overseas Chinese Relief Fund Committee, Siak Kew must have been swamped with managing these events and accounts of the donations which came in from people from all walks of life. By the end of the year, slightly over $1.5 million Straits dollars was raised and sent back to China.[17] These fund-raising efforts to support China continued in Singapore, and the efforts were consolidated with the Southeast Asia Federation of China Relief Funds, abbreviated to Nanyang Federation, formed in October 1938.[18]

A few days after Britain declared war on the Axis powers, the Malaya Patriotic Fund was started on 7 September 1939 to support Britain's war efforts.[19] The Chinese section of the Malaya Patriotic Fund, Singapore branch, met under the leadership of then President of Chinese Chamber of Commerce, Lee Kong Chian (李光前), in late September 1939. Siak Kew was once again nominated a member of the committee in charge of fund-raising for war relief efforts.[20] Though they were still concerned with the plight of their friends and families back in China, the committee did their best and by the end of the year, raised an impressive $130,978.[21] The following year, Siak Kew once again demonstrated that his charitable spirit went beyond ethnic boundaries, when he contributed $500 to the War Fund in June, organised by *The Straits Times* to support the British war effort. He also contributed a modest $20, more than the minimal $11.11, for Poppy Day in November, to aid victims of air raids in Britain.[22]

His public spirit and skill at organising the community was not overlooked. He was appointed one of the fifteen war tax assessors

No. 1110.—THE WAR TAX ORDINANCE, 1941.
(No. 3 of 1941).

In exercise of the powers conferred upon him by the War Tax Ordinance, 1941, and all other powers thereunto him enabling, the Governor in Council hereby appoints the following gentlemen as Assessors under Section 3 (4) of the said Ordinance:—

DIVISION OF SINGAPORE.

Mr. L. W. Geddes;
Mr. R. A. Dix;
Mr. H. R. Aaron;
Mr. J. A. Elias;
Hon. Capt. Noor Mohamed Hashim bin Mohamed Dali, I.S.O.;
Mr. Heah Wing Chew;
Mr. Tan Hoon Siang;
Mr. Ng Sen Choy;
Mr. Ong Piah Teng;
Mr. Balactru Govindasamy;
Mr. O. Ramasamy Nadar;
Mr. Fida Hussein Mohamedali Nakhoda;
Mr. Lim Kho Leng;
Mr. Tan Siak Kew;
Che Daud bin Mohamed Shah.

DIVISION OF PENANG.

Mr. E. C. Martin;
Mr. P. A. Abdul Ghaffoor;
Mr. C. B. Kamdar;
Mr. Lim Keong Lay;
Mr. Lim Lean Teng.

DIVISION OF MALACCA.

Mr. A. J. Boynton;
Mr. C. F. Gomes;
Mr. Tan Eng Chye;
Mr. Tan Soo Ghi.

Council Chamber,
Singapore, 26th March, 1941.
[No. C.S.O. 1165/41].

K. H. BANCROFT,
Clerk of Councils.

Figure 7.   Straits Settlements Gazette Notification No. 1110, announcing Siak Kew as Assessor under War Tax Ordinance of 1941.
Source: Straits Settlements Gazettes, CO276/159.

by the colonial government in May 1941. It was a privilege to have been selected, amongst other heavy-weights, including the general manager of the Oversea-Chinese Banking Corporation (OCBC), Ong Piah Teng (王丙丁), descendants of notable Chinese such as Tan Hoon Siang, a descendant of noted philantrophist Tan Tock Seng, and Lim Kho Leng, son of Lim Boon Keng.[23] It was not an enviable task though. The War Tax Ordinance passed with some heated debate in the Legislative Council, especially because local merchants feared that this income-based tax will become permanent in the future.[24] Tay Lian Teck (郑连德), an unofficial member of the Legislative Council, urged for Asiatic representation on the panel of assessors to protect them from 'unfair treatment of unnecessary inquisition', an abuse of power which reared its ugly head when a war tax was introduced during the last war.[25] As an assessor, Siak Kew thus fulfilled a crucial role of mediating these possible conflicts between the colonial government's Collector and the Chinese merchants who might be subjected to unfair harassment due to their different method of bookkeeping. The difficulties of this war tax were, however, to be superseded by Siak Kew's experiences when Singapore fell under the spectre of Japanese Occupation, in February 1942.

Under the Red Sun

In 1942, Siak Kew and his family spent their reunion dinner on Chinese New Year's Eve in their home at Keng Lee Road with some trepidation. The Japanese air force had commenced bombing raids on Singapore since 8 December 1941. While newspapers might have remained deceptively optimistic about the British ability to hold off the invading Japanese, few locals believed them. The most prominent leader of the China Relief Fund, Tan Kah Kee, had left Singapore before the official invasion on 8 February 1942. On 15 February 1942, instead of a riotous celebration of Chinese New Year, it was a day of subdued palpitation, as the British officially surrendered to the Japanese. Chinese New Year was the furthest on Siak Kew's mind as he fretted over possible reprisals from the new Japanese overlords.

Indeed, revenge against the overseas Chinese who had supported anti-Japanese activities in China was one of the priorities of the Japanese military administration. In the succeeding days following the fall of Singapore, Operation Sook Ching (肅清), or Dai Kensho in Japanese, meaning 'great inspection', was launched. The motive of the inspection was to identify and eliminate Chinese males between ages 18 and 50 who were members of the volunteer force, communist, looters, possessors of arms, and those whose names were found in lists of anti-Japanese suspects maintained by Japanese intelligence.[26]

Unlike the 50,000 Chinese who were shot in places such as Punggol Beach, Changi Beach, and Tanah Merah, Siak Kew escaped the death sentence. But he was detained by Japanese officers for a few weeks.[27] Yap Pheng Geck, a Teochew banker, described the conditions of detention at the Tanjong Pagar Police Station:

> [W]e were thrown into the lock-up together with other detainees —
> 40 to 50 people in all. There was not a stick of furniture in this place.
> We only had the cement floor to sit or lie on all day and night. Among
> the other detainees crammed within the lock-up were Sir Han Hoe
> Lim, Lee Wee Nam, Yeo Chan Boon, Tan Siak Kew, Ching Kee San,
> and other leading members of the Chinese business community. There
> was only one lavatory and when the water supply failed, the condition
> was appalling. We were caged in like beasts awaiting the slaughter. We
> could not understand what was going on or what was in store for us.[28]

Siak Kew was detained for three weeks but was eventually released, much to the relief of his family.[29] In exchange for his freedom, he had to join the Overseas Chinese Association (OCA), made up of both Straits-born and Chinese-born business and community leaders.

The OCA had the unenviable task of raising $12.5 million for the Japanese government in a month. Formed on 2 March, with the eminent Straits Chinese Lim Boon Keng as the President and the prominent Cantonese S.Q. Wong as the Vice-President, the OCA met at Goh Loo Club (吾庐俱乐部), located at Club Street. Siak Kew joined the 6th meeting on 15 March, which discussed mainly the need to account for the various members of individual clan associations.[31] In a subsequent 19 March meeting, it was decided that three Teochew representatives will be

Figure 8.   Image of Overseas Chinese Association, taken on 1 May 1942. Siak Kew is in the second row (fourth from the right).[30]
Source: Image courtesy of Mr Tan Puay Hiang.

Figure 9.   Goh Loo Club, where the OCA held its meetings.
Source: Lee Kip Lin collection, courtesy of National Library Board.

elected to the Council of Management, and Siak Kew was one of them.[32] The Japanese officers bore a grudging attitude towards the OCA, knowing that many of its members had contributed to the China Relief Fund, and the new Japanese masters were certainly not afraid to show their dissatisfaction with the Chinese leaders. Siak Kew himself was warned by a Japanese official of the Special Branch to stop speaking English if he wanted to keep his head.[33]

If the British colonial government's 1941 War Tax Ordinance had been a burden to businessmen, the ones which the OCA had been forced to implement were certainly much worse. Instead of

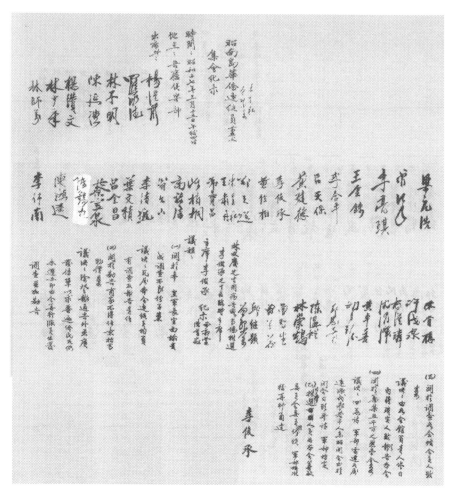

Figure 10.   Meeting minutes of the OCA meeting which Siak Kew first attended. His signature is third from left in the second row.
Source: Chua Ser-Koon and Hsu Yun-Tsiao (eds.), *Malayan Chinese Resistance to Japan 1937–1945: Selected Source Materials Based on Colonel Chuang Hui-Tsuan's Collection* (Singapore: Cultural & Historical Pub. House, 1984), p. 379.

progressive rates from 2 to 8 per cent based on annual incomes greater than $4,800, the OCA had decided that Chinese who owned property worth more than $3,000 had to pay a levy of 8 per cent of their assets.[34] Despite the harsh taxation, and several extensions of deadlines, the Malayan Overseas Chinese Association, made up of representatives from various states in Malaya, met up on 20 June in Singapore and realised they had only managed to raise $28 million, a far cry from the $50 million promised. On 25 June, the onerous task was finally completed with a loan of $22 million at 6 per cent interest from the Yokohama Specie Bank.[35] By this time, Siak Kew had stopped turning up for OCA meetings, suggesting that he had probably left the association and kept a low profile.[36] Siak Kew did not carry on his trading business, and lived quietly with Choon Siang and his seven children.[37] By this time, the family had relocated from their house at Keng Lee Road to the Buan Lee Seng premises at Fisher Street in Boat Quay.[38]

The Red Sun Sets

After three years and eight months of Japanese Occupation, the Japanese surrendered to the British on 12 September 1945 and life for Siak Kew gradually returned to normal. Before Siak Kew could return to his pre-war role as trader and Chinese business leader and leave the painful memories of the war behind, he joined the Appeal Committee for Singapore Chinese Victims Massacred by Japanese. Consisting of 37 prominent Chinese leaders, led by Hokkien businessman Tay Koh Yat (郑古悦), the Appeal Committee investigated the losses of the victims, excavated remains of victims, and spoke up to the British military administration during the War Crimes Tribunal to ensure that the losses of the Chinese were to be redressed. Under the leadership of Tay Koh Yat, the Appeal Committee had collected evidence for the prosecution, and were not afraid to voice their dissatisfaction with the death sentence of two out of the seven Japanese military officials on trial for the Chinese massacres.[39]

While the grievances of the Chinese would never quite be resolved after such a traumatic collective experience, with it resurfacing in the 1960s,[40] the end of war crimes trials was a temporary closure for some. For the time being, Siak Kew had to rebuild his life and business, in a political climate which would turn out to be markedly different from the pre-war period.

Sojourners to Settlers

We have made our homes and fortunes here and we want to stay here. Large sums are invested in Singapore by many Chinese who, because they were born in China, are now regarded as aliens, with no voting privileges and cannot get naturalisation papers. We have made our homes here; our children were born here; and our life's interests are in this colony. We feel that the time is now ripe to urge government to consider allowing us the privileges now only enjoyed by local-born Chinese.

— *Tan Siak Kew's comment in 1951 on the need to transform these China-born Chinese from sojourners to settlers*[vi]

[vi] "Give Franchise to China-born Chinese in Singapore Plea," *The Straits Times*, 6 January 1951, p. 5.

Singapore was, and perhaps still can be considered, a nation built by immigrants. While these tended to be sojourners, who would work in Singapore for a few years before returning to their countries of origin, the changes in international politics in the post-war period forced many of them to settle permanently in Singapore. For the Chinese, the Chinese Communist Party's victory in 1949 was a decisive turning point. Siak Kew saw Singapore as home early on. And he also worked hard to ensure that other sojourners could settle, through his position as Chinese Chamber of Commerce President speaking on citizenship and language debates in the 1950s, his position as a nominated member of the Legislative Assembly, and his position as a respected leader in the various community groups.

Citizenship and Language

While the Chinese Chamber of Commerce is today thought of as an organisation predominantly concerned with issues of trade, it had been active in political and social issues in the immediate aftermath of the war. George William Skinner, who was then attached with the Cornell Southeast Asia Programme, had this to say of the Chinese Chamber of Commerce after a research trip to Southeast Asia after the war:

> [The Chamber was] the largest and most important Chinese organisation in all of Southeast Asia ... The undisputed leader of the whole Chinese community, it takes up matters that are larger than the scope of any one regional or trade organisation.[41]

One such matter was the question of citizenship for the Chinese population. This issue, brought to the fore with new British regulations introduced in 1950 and intended to limit the flow of Chinese to and fro Singapore with the formation of the People's Republic of China in October 1949,[42] troubled the Chamber for a good decade.

Citizenship in Singapore, following the British system, was *jus soli*, meaning citizenship based on the soil on which one was born. However, China's citizenship policy was *jus sanguinis*, meaning citizenship based on descent. This meant that majority of the China-born Chinese residing in Singapore — about 250,000 in 1950 — were not citizens by birth and had to acquire it by naturalisation. They could only obtain citizenship via naturalisation by showing (1) an extended period of residence for at least four of the seven preceding years; (2) proof of good character; (3) sufficient knowledge of the English language; (4) intent to reside in the United Kingdom or any of its colonies or protectorates in the foreseeable future; and (5) declaring allegiance to the British crown.[43]

Siak Kew and his fellow members in the Singapore Chinese Chamber of Commerce were not blind to the plight of the Chinese in Singapore. In 1950, together with other prominent Chinese business leaders such as Tan Lark Sye (陈六使), Lee Kong Chian, and Tan Chin Tuan, he drew up a memorandum to urge the Singapore government to grant citizenship rights to these China-born Chinese.

Speaking to *The Straits Times*, then a paper which was published by and for the pro-colonial establishment, Siak Kew made an especially moving statement on this issue:

> Times have changed and our hearts are now no longer with a China dominated by Chinese Communists. We have made our homes and fortunes here and we want to stay here. Large sums are invested in Singapore by many Chinese who, because they were born in China, are now regarded as aliens, with no voting privileges and cannot get naturalisation papers. We have made our homes here; our children were born here; and our life's interests are in this colony. We feel that the time is

now ripe to urge government to consider allowing us the privileges now only enjoyed by local-born Chinese. Over the decades, domiciled Chinese have proved by their industry and sincerity that the development and progress of Singapore do no depend alone on the efforts of a favoured few, but on the majority. Naturalisation formalities are still too restrictive for those who do not speak or write English.[44]

Siak Kew was characteristically cautious with the framing of the statement, asking the British to expand upon pre-existing naturalisation laws rather than propose new citizenship criteria, even going to the lengths of citing a precedent when naturalisation was granted to the late former President of the Chinese Chamber of Commerce, Yong Yit Lin (杨溢麟), who did not speak or write English.

His Chamber colleagues, were, however, less willing to play by the existing British rules. The Chamber's Management Committee meeting in February 1951 saw the passing of a draft petition which was not content with merely relaxing naturalisation requirements, but proposed new requirements for local citizenship. These included (1) eight years of residency in the previous ten years; (2) declaration of no intention to leave for the next five years unless for business or vacation; (3) declaration of loyalty to colony; (4) undertaking not to declare allegiance to any foreign party, government, or state during period of residence in colony; and (5) ability to read Chinese or English.[45]

While these terms seem perfectly uncontroversial today, they were unpalatable to the British. For one, the declaration of loyalty to colony rather than the Queen was firmly rejected by Colonial Secretary W. Blythe, who saw it as an attempt to obtain 'full citizenship rights for the China-born in return for a declaration of temporary allegiance'.[46] Even British officials who were not trapped in the illusion of a never-ending colonial rule in Singapore were hesitant to accept these terms. Under Malayan pressure not to give rights to people who were not naturalised British subjects, they did not wish to jeopardise their decolonisation plans, which included a future merger between Malaya and Singapore. Siak Kew's caution was clearly not unfounded.

A small compromise was made, when the British removed the language clause for the acquisition of British citizenship via naturalisation in December 1951. However, the Chamber was not satisfied.[47] It continued its fight for citizenship, not just naturalised subject status. In 1952, a motion was raised to send a memorandum to the colonial government, a motion which Siak Kew finally agreed to, but not without cautioning that the British had replied the Chamber earlier this year with both rational and reasonable explanations, and that a minor concession had been made in permitting non-English speakers to be naturalised.[48] The Chamber had approached Tan Cheng Lock to help persuade the colonial government once again in 1953, but to no avail.[49]

The results of the Rendel Commission, led by Sir George Rendel to make recommendations on the Constitution of Singapore to pave the way for self-governance, were to further complicate the Chamber's cause in 1954. Firstly, it abolished the century-old principle of representation of trade on the legislative body, an issue which will be discussed further in the next chapter. Secondly, and more relevant to the discussion of citizenship, power was to be transferred from the colonial government to the Legislative Assembly made up of officials mainly elected by the public.[50] The issue of citizenship was now intricately tied up with that of electoral representation and voice.

In November 1954, the Chamber started an electioneering committee, launching a series of rallies in 1955 to persuade voters to register and go to the polls. Seven 'use your votes' rallies were held, costing the Chamber only $858 as the individual Chamber leaders had borne the costs.[51] Siak Kew was silent on the issue, and never participated in these rallies, not because he did not believe in the importance of voter registration, but likely because he was uncomfortable with the Chamber flirting so closely with political participation. This belief in separation of business with partisan politics will be discussed in greater detail in the next chapter.

Political Representation

Though Siak Kew refrained from participating in the voter registration campaigns, this did not mean he was not concerned with political representation. After the 1955 elections, the Chamber picked up on another issue which was close to the hearts of the Chinese community — language. In late 1954, the Chamber had sent a petition asking for the Legislative Assembly to be multi-lingual, which was an issue closely linked to the expansion of political participation to the non-English educated. In August 1955, a ten-men delegation from the Chamber, including Siak Kew, met with Colonial Secretary Alan Lennox Boyd, Chief Minister David Marshall, and Chief Secretary W. A. C. Goode, to discuss the issue of citizenship and the acceptance of other languages in future Assembly proceedings.[52] They had, in the words of the colonial officials, 'presented their case skilfully', though the Secretary ultimately decided to leave the matter to the Singapore government.[53]

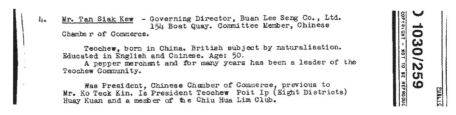

Figure 11. In preparation for the meeting with the Chamber delegates, a dossier was compiled by the colonial office. Siak Kew's entry was brief, about half the length compared to the other members, such as Tan Lark Sye or Ko Teck Kin. Presumably, Siak Kew did not worry the British officials as much.
Source: 'Biological Notes of Members of Delegation to see the Secretary of State on 18.8.55 in Connection with Singapore Citizenship Question,' CO 1030/259.

Siak Kew had a real shot at ensuring fairer political representation when he was nominated member of the Legislative Assembly in 1958. In one of his earliest speeches, which was a comment on Governor William Goode's Opening Speech, he summarised his belief that the nation must take precedence over petty politics, and businessmen were an important component of the new nation:

> In fact, most businessmen have not much interest as to who is to govern next but they would certainly like to see that, whichever party comes into power, it has a sense of responsibility as expressed in the Governor's Speech — a sense of responsibility to the livelihood of all of the people here and not to one section of the people. As I say, most of the businessmen have built up their businesses here from scratch. Most of them were labourers and clerks before. By dint of hard work, they were able to achieve whatever they have now and if there is any sign that Singapore would be destroyed because of politics, then those who are most able to — the biggest ones — will be running away and those who cannot afford to run away, I am quite sure, will fight for their lives. Therefore, I should like all political parties to bear this point in mind, that the livelihood of the people — capitalists, the average businessman, and every section of the people — should be guarded and not destroyed.[54]

It was as if Siak Kew was talking about himself, his experiences of building up his business from scratch here in Singapore and settling down here, staying on during the Japanese Occupation instead of running away, and now, as nominated member of the Legislative Assembly, arguing for how government ought to protect the interests of all, and not just a select few. Aside from being a passionate speaker for business interests (see next chapter for more), he also spoke up for education and Nanyang University (see education chapter).

Light of Teochews

Siak Kew was known for his contributions to the Teochew community, contributing actively to clan-based organisations such as the

Figure 12. The Federated Teochew Association of Malaysia (马来亚潮州公会联合会) of 31 Teochew dialect-based organisations across Singapore and the Malay Peninsula, honoured Siak Kew with this gold-embossed laquer plaque, which measured 183cm by 76cm. Celebrating his appointment as Singapore's first Ambassador to Thailand, it proclaimed Siak Kew as the Light of Teochews.
Source: Photo taken at Mr Tan Puay Hiang's home, by Fiona Tan.

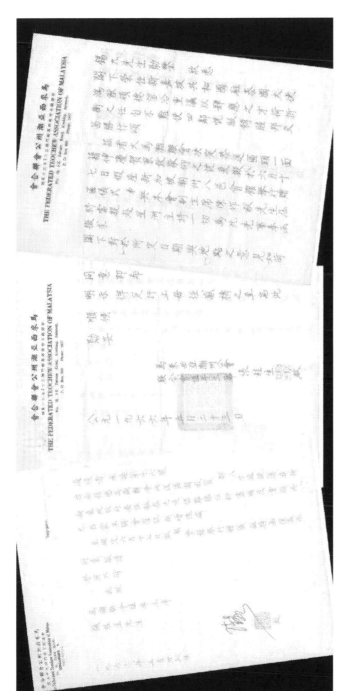

Figure 13.   Letters between the Federated Teochew Association of Malaysia and Siak Kew in May 1966 regarding his appointment as Ambassador to Thailand and the awarding of the plaque to Siak Kew. Ever the humble man, Siak Kew's response was that he was only performing his national duty.

Source: Image courtesy of Mr Tan Puay Hiang.

Ngee Ann Kongsi and Teochew Poit Ipp Huay Kuan, both organisations which were dedicated to helping Teochew sojourners settle down in Singapore.

The Teochew Poit Ipp Huay Kuan traces its history back to 1928, when a group of prominent Teochew businessmen, including Siak Kew's father-in-law Leow Chia Heng, decided to found a Teochew community association in reaction to what they considered an increasingly Seah Eu Chin-dominated Ngee Ann Kongsi.[55] Housed in Tuan Mong School at Tank Road, the Teochew Poit Ipp Huay Kuan represented the interests of members from the eight Teochew districts — Teo Ann (潮安), Chenghai (澄海), Chaoyang (潮阳), Jieyang (揭阳), Raoping (饶平), Puning (普宁), Huilai (惠来), and Nan'ao (南澳). Its early leaders consisted of pioneers of the likes of Lim Nee Soon, Lee Wee Nam, and Yeo Chan Boon, with a member strength of 700 within its first year of founding. By September 1929, the two organisations reconciled with each other upon the restructuring of Ngee Ann Kongsi, and have since been closely associated, with the Kongsi acting as a trustee's organisation and providing funds to maintain the Huay Kuan.[56] A key organisation which helped Teochew immigrants settle down in Singapore, in the postwar period, as the population became more domiciled, it focused its attention on the provision of educational facilities, charity, and the promotion of arts and culture. Siak Kew was a long-serving leader of this organisation, having served as the Treasurer, a Director on its Board, Vice-President, President, and Honorary President.[57]

Siak Kew was also active in the Ngee Ann Kongsi, serving as its 18th President for a short period of two months between April to June 1965. A public spat between two factions of the Ngee Ann Kongsi's Board of Governors was the reason behind Siak Kew's sudden resignation. It first began in late May 1965, when Siak Kew requested for the halting of works on a multi-million dollar expansion of Ngee Ann College's site in Clementi to house its new

Department of Technology.[58] Siak Kew was concerned that the Kongsi was spending funds it did not have and misleading students and their families by expanding a College which had yet to gain formal recognition from the government. The faction for the continuation of the building had resigned from the Board of the College in protest, and over 1,000 students staged a two-day boycott of classes.[59]

In the end, for the sake of the students and to keep the Kongsi's commitment to the construction company, Siak Kew gave in and

Figure 14. Ngee Ann Students boycotted classes at the main campus on Tank Road against what they described as an 'evasive attitude' of the Ngee Ann Kongsi's Committee led by Siak Kew.
Source: Straits Times © Singapore Press Holdings Ltd. Reprinted with permission.

persuaded the members of those against the construction of the College to follow suit.[60] However, feeling as though he may let the community down by spending money which the Kongsi did not have, he resigned.[61]

Beyond *Bangs*

While Siak Kew was certainly active in contributing to the dialect-based organisations such as those described above, the potential flipside was that he might have also been used as an exemplar of someone who perpetuated dialect bias. At the 1987 National Day Rally, Siak Kew was raised as an example of a typical Chinese who still held on to dialect-based discriminatory beliefs:

> I was once at a wedding, the Chinese Chamber of Commerce, where a Teochew gentleman (Siak Kew) who was once a High Commissioner in Kuala Lumpur [sic: it was clarified in a corrigendum published the following day that Siak Kew was Ambassador to Thailand] invited me ... And he had all his sons lined up ... His number one son, his wife, Hokkien, not so good. You know, but he didn't say not so good but from the face; you know this. Then, another son. Oh this is even worse because she doesn't look Chinese. This is very bad. Then he says, Ah, this last one. This new daughter-in-law, she's Teochew. That he thoroughly approved of![62]

However, this comment must be viewed in its context, as then Prime Minister Lee Kuan Yew had probably said this in jest. It was to illustrate the dialect-based differentiation in the Chinese communities, and was not a statement of fact on Siak Kew's personality. Indeed, Siak Kew had shown that he was above dialect differences, not only through his personal friendships with prominent Hokkiens such as Ko Teck Kin (高德根), but also through his public actions.

One such example was in 1952, when a faction of predominantly Hokkien members of the Singapore Chinese Chamber of Commerce raised the notion of eliminating the *bang* structure in the Chamber.[63] The *bang* system, basically meant a politico-socio-economic grouping based principally on dialect groups, not surprising given the divergent geographical origins of Singaporean Chinese. The main dialect groups in Singapore were the Hokkiens, Teochews, Cantonese, Hakka, and Hainanese, each occupying a niche area of the economy. In the context of the Chinese Chamber of Commerce, the *bang* system meant an election system based on the proportionate representation of the various dialect groups.

The challenge posed by the Hokkien faction led by Colonel Chuang Hui-Tsuan was not simply driven by any romantic notion of unifying the Chinese community, but also by pragmatic reasons of trying to ensure that the KMT supporters within the Hokkien community were given a chance to enter the Management Committee. He couched it in terms of eliminating competition among the various *bang* organisations and to create opportunities for younger members who were disadvantaged by the fixed quotas of members who could be elected based on the size of their dialect groups.[64] Siak Kew, together with the other members of the Management Committee, were against that for fear that it would disadvantage the minority dialect groups like the Sanjiang, and this motion was dropped.

Helping sojourners settle through his powerful position as President of the Chinese Chamber of Commerce, leader of the various dialect-based community organisations, and a nominated member of the Legislative Assembly was Siak Kew's key contribution to the building of the nation. However, Siak Kew was a trader by profession, and to him, trade was an integral part of Singapore. It is to his business philosophy that we now turn to.

Business is Not Politics

主席乃起谓余觉得关于章程之辩论完全係因吾人对商会之立场有两种不同之见解。其一认为商会係本坡八十万华侨之最高机关，一切有关华侨事务皆本会职责所在；另一则认为本会不过各帮侨商之集团。吾人在商言商，有关华侨之商务为本会份内应理之事，其他事物须能力所及方可兼顾。

This debate over the Chamber's Constitution stems from two distinct stances on the role of the Chamber. One believes that the Chamber is the most important organisation for Singapore's 80,000 Chinese, and is hence responsible for all things to do with the community. The second believes this Chamber is only a coalition of the various *bang* organisations. I believe we should only talk about business here, and only concern ourselves with matters which affect the commercial aspects of the Chinese community.

— *Tan Siak Kew explaining the* 在商言商 *role of the Chamber in society*[vii]

[vii] 在商言商 means "when in business, discuss business", Singapore Chinese Chamber of Commerce (SCCC) meeting minutes, 17 June 1952.

The Chinese have a saying, "在商言商", which literally means when in business, discuss business. For all his sense of social responsibility to community and nation, Siak Kew was especially cautious not to mix politics — especially the deeply dividing partisan politics — with business.

Politics in post-war Singapore was fractured along deep fissures. Race and political ideologies converged, making the British colonial masters deeply suspicious and reluctant to work with the Chinese in the grand masterplan of eventual, albeit very gradual, decolonisation. The victory of the Communist Party in China, and the State of Emergency imposed in Malaya against the guerrilla fighters of the Malayan Communist Party, only made the British more suspicious of the large Chinese community. And that included the business community.

Staying Out of China's Politics

Unlike some of his more vocal peers, Siak Kew always took a non-partisan approach to tackling issues within the Chinese Chamber of Commerce and never publicly expressed his political opinions.[65] Unlike Tan Kah Kee, who held a meeting at the Chinese Chamber of Commerce in late September 1946 to draft a four-point resolution supporting his recent cable to President Truman urging the US to cease support for what he felt was a corrupt Kuomintang government, Siak Kew resolutely stayed out of China's politics. Together with thirteen members of the new Committee of the Singapore Chinese Chamber of Commerce, Siak Kew resigned from the Chamber. Protesting against 'misuse of the Chamber premises', they feared the use of the premises for purposes such as Tan Kah Kee's recent meeting might foster an erroneous impression that the Chamber was 'dabbling in politics'.[66] It was more of a symbolic

Figure 15. Newly elected as the Vice-President of the Chinese Chamber of Commerce to President Tan Lark Sye, Siak Kew would prove to be a moderating force in the Chamber, advocating for businessmen to contribute to nationhood without becoming embroiled in partisan politics.
Source: Straits Times © Singapore Press Holdings Ltd. Reprinted with permission.

gesture, as they withdrew their resignations two days later.[67] However, the extremes they went to, tendering resignations just days after the induction of the new committee, was testament to their resolute belief that the Chamber of Commerce had to stay out of politics.

Nor was this symbolic protest an indication of Siak Kew's political beliefs. In 1951, when the Associated Chinese Chambers of Commerce of Malaya (马华商联会) proposed a letter to the British colonial government to deny recognition to Communist China, Siak Kew was one of those who objected to it. Reminding the Singapore Chinese Chamber of Commerce of their mandate to keep business and politics separate, Siak Kew agreed with then President, Tan Lark Sye, that the Chamber should not be embroiled in politics.[68]

Experimenting with Politics

In 1952, in response to Colonel Chuang's threatened resignation over his proposal to eliminate the *bang* structure in the Chamber, Siak Kew made an impassioned speech, as President, explaining his view of the role the Chamber ought to play:

> 主席乃起谓余觉得关于章程之辩论完全係因吾人对商会之立场有两种不同之见解。其一认为商会係本坡八十万华侨之最高机关，一切有关华侨事务皆本会职责所在；另一则认为本会不过各帮侨商之集团。吾人在商言商，有关华侨之商务为本会份内应理之事，其他事物须能力所及方可兼顾。以余之见如各董事採取第一种见解，认为华人一切事物本会均应办理，则本会会员既纯属商人，不能网罗各方面之人才，难以应付一切事务。应即改组，使组织瑧于健全，需要时本人亦愿让贤。如採取第二种见解，则吾人只有在可能范围内尽办理一切事项。

> This debate over the Chamber's Constitution stems from two distinct stances on the role of the Chamber. One believes that the Chamber is the most important organisation for Singapore's 80,000 Chinese, and is hence responsible for all things to do with the community. The second believes this Chamber is only a coalition of the various *bang* organisations. I believe we should only talk about business here, and only concern ourselves with matters which affect the commercial aspects of the Chinese community. To members who take the first interpretation of what role the Chamber ought to play, and believe that the Chamber should concern itself with all things Chinese, I want to point out that the Chamber consists only of businessmen, and not experts in other fields, so the Chamber can hardly handle other issues. To pursue that path, the Chamber needs to reorganise and revamp itself entirely, and I will be most willing to step aside. If the Chamber takes the second interpretation of its role, I will humbly do my best to resolve issues relevant to commerce.[69]

Though Siak Kew had proven that he was sometimes willing to use his position in society to advise on issues not related to commerce, such as in the very crucial citizenship issue, his stance on keeping business and partisan politics distinct was very much in line with his non-confrontational style of leadership. While he managed to keep the Chamber out of partisan politics during his period of presidency, the new Management Committee elected in 1954 was less concerned with participating in politics.

In 1954, the Rendel Commission recommended the removal of a nominated member on the legislature from the various Chambers of Commerce. Instead, the business community will be represented on the Trade Advisory Board, which would then make recommendations to the elected Minister of Trade. The Chinese Chamber of Commerce was naturally all ablaze with discussions over that. Sharing the sentiments of his fellow Chamber members and their counterparts from the other Chambers of Commerce, Siak Kew stated in no uncertain terms that it was 'highly presumptuous for the Commission to believe that trade representation could adequately be met by elected members of political parties.'[70]

Siak Kew was not convinced that direct involvement in partisan politics was the best way to restore the voice of the Chambers of Commerce in the legislature. Elected officials were obliged to serve the welfare of the broader community and not just focus on matters related to trade and commerce, as critical as they were to nation-building. In his view, industry representatives in the legislature were best placed to give objective advice to politicians, when they themselves did not become politicians.

At the first meeting of the 28th Committee of the Singapore Chinese Chamber of Commerce on 26 March 1954, the new President Ko Teck Kin raised the possibility of the Chamber supporting candidates at City or Legislative Council elections. The meeting minutes recorded Siak Kew's cautious response:

陈锡九在原则上亦主张商会应协助能为公众谋福利者竞选市委及立委，但认此举如沦为政党或与其他政党作竞敌对立场，则应考虑。

Tan Siak Kew agreed on principle that the Chamber should support electoral candidates who are concerned about the welfare of the public, but believes that if this leads to the Chamber's involvement in partisan politics and having to oppose other political parties, it should reconsider.[71]

The Chamber, now in a period of its history which historian Sikko Visscher considers to be the 'high point of ambition', entered popular politics in response to the threat of the lack of trade representation on the Legislative Assembly.[72] A thinly veiled allusion to the privileged background of its members, the Democratic Party (DP), was more widely known as 'The Millionaires' Party'.[73] Led by Teochew businessman, Tan Ek Khoo, the DP received strong

Figure 16.   Election posters for the 1955 Legislative Assembly elections, where the Chinese Chamber of Commerce was taught the painful lesson of being embroiled unnecessarily in popular politics.
Source: Courtesy of National Archives of Singapore, Ministry of Information and the Arts Collection.

financial backing from prominent businessmen such as Tan Kah Kee. Fielding far more businessmen among its candidates for the Legislative Assembly elections than any other political party, the DP naturally had business interests on its mind, with a manifesto that had free trade high on its priorities. Echoing the concerns of the Chamber, it also supported the development of Nanyang University, and for a multi-lingual Legislative Assembly. It was simply a Chinese communal party, as some historians have characterised it as.[74] It, however, clearly failed to garner sufficient popular support, winning only two out of the twenty seats it contested.[75]

Though the Democratic Party was never officially endorsed by the Chamber — the Chamber in fact went to great lengths to dispute the allegations that they were associated[76] — contemporaneous sources, such as newspapers, as well as posthumous histories have acknowledged a very strong link between these two organisations. In an Election Forum over Radio Malaya on 24 March 1955, David Marshall even cheekily joked that the DP had shifted headquarters to the Chinese Chamber of Commerce when the DP candidate insisted that he had no knowledge of the rich men's club — Ee Hoe Hean Club.[77] The point here is not to prove or disprove the relationship, but that this failed experimentation with direct participation in politics, was proof that Siak Kew, and others who shared his cautiousness, were not far off the mark when they cautioned the Chamber from getting embroiled in politics.

No Trade, No State

Maintaining a strict distinction between business and politics, however, does not necessarily imply a lack of concern for broader issues. Indeed, one of Siak Kew's more verbose speeches as recorded in the Chamber's meeting minutes was a rare display of his disagreement with the policies of the Labour Front-led coalition government in 1956:

主席至此对于新政府之法令即提出批评，称当林德限制拟取消立法议会中中、西、印三商会席位时，吾人曾大加反对。原因星市繁荣全靠商业，如商业不振，工界亦必同蒙不利，故新政府一切法令如有不利于商家，势必影响工商业，造成失业浪潮。如政府只欲实现其政治理想，通过一些法令，虽然取得一般不顾事实者之同情，工商界已大受打击矣。

如以公积金一事而论，其理想係为工人利益，但实施后却遭工人与店员之反对，甚至希望其取消。而且通过一新令，必须多用一批公务员，增加纳税人负担。公积金如战前有此制度，假如现在有人领得五千元之公积金，其币值较战前如何？就现在几下公积金，三、二十年后其币值较现在又如何？此纯为一种众敛政策，于是即毫无益处。

冻结地价法令实施当然又多一机构，多用一批公务员。而且买卖地产又要有估价馆估价，向官方请示价格是否公正，方能成交。但估价馆与政府批准是否无弊？买卖应按需求原理，如实行该法令适以阻碍当地今后之发展。

关于店员书记法令，星市地小人多，人口又日告加增。一切施政应随人口而着力工商业之发展，使人任由工做，人人生活能安定。当地生意多係小规模，日夕奋斗仅能维持生活而已。稍受法令束缚便无法经营，影响所及失业分子徒增。本地既无金山又无银矿，商业繁荣一向仅仰仗与邻邦之转口贸易。故凡以此地为家乡者，应先注意发展当地工商业。

所得税方面，过去所得税係生命应守秘密；今则马氏建议应公布纳税人名单，完全违背当日原则。总之当地政府如以人民福利为前提，则应接纳吾人意见。如仅将有利政治理想一意孤行、舍本逐末，则将来对于本地工商业均有不利。

The President aired his criticisms towards the new government. When the Rendel Commission recommended the removal of nominated representatives from the three Chambers of Commerce, the President strongly objected. The reason was because Singapore's prosperity was entirely dependent on trade. If trade declined, the industries will be affected. If the new legislations harmed trade, it will have an effect on industries and cause unemployment. If the present government only thinks about political aims, and passes some legislation to win over the less informed, Singapore's industries will be badly affected.

The new Central Provident Fund Bill is an example in point, which ideally is to the benefit of workers but in reality, was resisted by workers. Moreover, this new legislation creates the need for a bureaucratic agency and civil servants, adding to taxpayers' burden. If there was such a scheme in place before the war, and a person could now withdraw $5000 from his Central Provident savings, how does it take into account the currency fluctuations over the years? Or compare it with 20, 30 years down the road? This is an example of a policy that panders to the public without having real benefits.

The proposal to freeze land prices also entails the formation of another agency and the hiring of another batch of civil servants. And it requires the evaluation of the land price to be approved by government before a transaction can occur. However, who can ensure that the evaluator and the government's judgement is fair? Transactions should be conducted rationally, and this legislation will undoubtedly affect the development of Singapore.

The Clerks and Shop Assistants Employment Bill is another one. Singapore is a small country with a growing population. Legislation should follow the development of industries, which support the employment of the growing population and fosters stability in society. Most of our businesses are small-scale, and they fight to break even. Adding more legislative red-tape will cripple them, and cause further unemployment. Singapore has neither gold mountains nor silver mines, and is heavily reliant on trade with neighbouring countries. If we truly view this place as home, we need to focus on developing local industries.

As for the new revisions to taxation practices. In the past, the name lists of those who were taxed were kept confidential. Now, Marshall suggests making it public and it goes against the principles of the initial tax legislations.

In conclusion, if the government places the public's welfare at the top of its priorities, it should seriously consider public feedback. If they simply pursue political aims and proceed without considering the implications, it will be detrimental to local trade and industries.[78]

Figure 17.   Siak Kew and Ng Quee Lam on their way to see Chief Minister Lim Yew Hock. As a rational and neutral member of the Chinese Chamber of Commerce, Siak Kew's views were trusted and sought-after by the government.
Source: Straits Times © Singapore Press Holdings Ltd. Reprinted with permission.

Siak Kew did not mince his words when he criticized the government. Evident from this speech was his indictment of government policies which appeared to pander to populist sentiment without having clear long-term benefits for society. Some of the critiques were addressed, albeit some time later. For instance, the Central Provident Fund Scheme was later tweaked to reflect market-rate interest rates in 1957.[79] Such constructive criticisms were one of the many voices which helped refine what would otherwise be merely populist gestures which sought to win over the electorate.

His strong belief in the connection between trade and state-building was not new, and was put forth as early as 1950, when he first objected to the possibility of the removal of Chamber of

Commerce representatives on the Legislative Assembly. Considering it 'a most tragic suggestion', he went as far as to state that 'without trade there is no Singapore, no government, no professions, no welfare or social services, no means of livelihood for the population.'[80]

In 1958, Siak Kew became the nominated member on the Legislative Assembly, and he exercised his responsibility of speaking up for state and business with vigour. His maiden speech on the Legislative Assembly on 23 April 1958 was a lengthy defence of how Singapore was heavily reliant on trade and that government has a 'responsibility to the livelihood of all of the people here and not to one section of the people.'[81] That was, however, not the pinnacle of his verbosity when it came to a defence of the business community. In the Legislative Assembly debates of 1958, over the matter of the Control of Manufacture Bill, Siak Kew went on an extensive speech which took up seven columns in the Legislative Assembly Debates Proceedings, lasted over five minutes, and had been interrupted twice by the Speaker who urged him to condense the newspaper quotations which he had used to support his point.[82]

Singapore was then a plural society consisting of various different communities. To Siak Kew, businesses were also important in overcoming traditional fissure lines in society. During his term as President in the Chinese Chamber of Commerce, his leadership style was said to be one of the more amenable to other dialect groups.[83] As long-serving President of the Chinese Produce Exchange (1948–1967), a trade dominated by Teochews and Hokkiens, Siak Kew was not only fluent in the various other dialects, he was also very much open to other nationalities given the exposure to them when doing trade.[84] He was also very much for the idea of fostering inter-racial understanding through the employment of non-Chinese into Chinese firms and factories, which would also provide for business-minded Malays to get experience from such firms before setting up their own businesses.[85] Such idealism was an expression of his belief in the key role business should play in state and nation-building.

From Trader to Banker

Siak Kew was a conservative business leader, and also a conservative businessman. Primarily a produce trader, having carved out his expertise while in Buan Mui Seng and bringing it to further heights in his own company, Buan Lee Seng, Siak Kew's tactful leadership style made him an ideal President of the Chinese Produce Exchange for 16 consecutive years. He was cautious as a businessman. Rumour has it that when Tan Lark Sye asked for his investment in a new venture, Siak Kew requested for a prospectus before committing any funds, which was rare in those days when businesses among friends were often conducted without contracts. At that table in Tanjong Rhu Club, Tan pulled out a crumpled piece of paper, with some scribblings describing the business, and handed it to Siak Kew. The contents of the paper or the outcome of the discussion were never made known, but this anecdote only serves to prove Siak Kew's cautious approach to business.[86]

While cautious, he was not a traditionalist. Sometimes, he took a bet on new technologies ahead of its time, such as participating in one of the largest industrial acquisitions of Cressonite Industries Ltd. in 1951.[87] While Cressonite Industries was founded and managed by L. Cresson, a notable rubber chemist based in Singapore since the 1920s, the industrial production of rubber and plastic products had yet to take off in pre-industrial Singapore.

Siak Kew was also willing to venture beyond his comfort zone of trading, and became a banker. Joining the Board of Directors in 1962, he took over the reins of Sze Hai Tong Bank (later known as Four Seas Communications Bank) after the death of Lee Wee Nam in 1964. Even as Siak Kew was adept in business, he had to assume the role of a lender when he became a financier. An anecdote from his son's contemporaries speaks of him also employing informal methods as a banker. At the Chui Huay Lim Club frequented by Teochews, this young man was initially worried as a man of Siak Kew's stature approached him, and that gave way to astonishment as the veteran leader sat before him and offered him a cigar. They exchanged some small talk, with the young lad clearly in awe that a man of Siak Kew's stature would come over to initiate conversation. Later, he realised that Siak Kew was trying to get information on the credit-standing of a company, and what better way to do so than through informal conversations with men of their generation. In the 1960s, when hierarchies were still very much respected, for the leader of the bank to be conducting such inquiries was an indication of Siak Kew's thoroughness in conducting his business. Four Seas Communications Bank was later merged with OCBC in 1972, following Tan Chin Tuan's unconditional offer to Siak Kew and an informal assurance that Four Seas would continue to operate as an independent subsidiary.

Siak Kew's business philosophy was both cautious and adventurous. He had a strong commitment to ensuring shareholders got their dues, and did not take unnecessary risks. However, this did not mean he was not willing to try new methods or make difficult and unpopular decisions. And he brought this same attitude into his leadership style, where he was conciliatory and non-partisan but with a firm belief that nation and the well-being of the population must come first. There can be no Singapore without trade, and his measured criticisms as President of the Chinese Chamber of Commerce was trusted and sought-after by the government.

The Nantah Experiment

人才是社会的栋梁，教育是国家的灵魂，大学尤其是人才荟萃的
中心，国家文化的宝库及国民生活的堡垒…东方的文化，历史悠
久，博大精深，重精神文明；西方文化，科学昌明，日新月异，
重物质文明；二者皆为世界文化的主流，而各有其优点，南洋大
学所在的新加坡又是在东西文化的交汇点，无疑的可以负起沟通
东西文化、融合贯通，採其精华，发扬光大，创造出独特性的东
西揉合的新加坡文化。南洋大学在目前还有一个特殊的任务，就
是对东方文化，东方民族的德行以及东方文化在学术上所特有的
优良传统，应该加以发扬，不但对沟通东西文化工作可以放射灿
烂的光辉，并且有助于世界文化的发展。

If human talent is the foundation of society and education is the soul
of nation, then the university is the centre for nurturing talent, the
safe for national culture, and the castle for its citizens … Chinese
culture has a long and profound history, with an emphasis on the
spiritual. Western culture is innovative and technologically advanced,
with an emphasis on the material. These two cultures have their own
unique contributions to the world. Nantah, located in Singapore
where both cultures converge, is thus in an ideal position to promote
the best of Chinese and Western cultures, and to create a unique
Singaporean culture. Nantah's special task now, is to preserve and

promote the best virtues and scholarship of Eastern traditions, which
will not only help in cross-cultural exchanges, but also aid in the
development of a truly global culture.

— *Tan Siak Kew, Convocation Address, 24 May 1969*[viii]

O n 24 May 1969, Siak Kew addressed the Minister of Education, Ong Pang Boon, the staff and students of Nantah
and their parents, for his fourth and final time as Chairman of the University Council, in the first convocation held in the
newly-built Nanyang University Auditorium. Coinciding with the
150th anniversary of Singapore, this convocation ceremony was the
tenth in Nantah's tumultous history. Aware of the milestones Nantah had passed and perhaps in light of his pending retirement from
the University Council the following year, Siak Kew had delivered
an extraordinarily long and poetic convocation address in Mandarin.[88] The short excerpt from that very speech, at the beginning of
this chapter, aptly summarises Siak Kew's philosophy towards education and the role it had in a young nation, and explains his dedica-
tion to Nantah's key role in providing a cross-cultural education
which combined the best from Chinese and Western traditions.

After all, he had served the University faithfully as Chairman of
the University Council since Ko Teck Kin's unexpected death in
April 1966. As Siak Kew was a close associate of then Chairman Ko,
and had been supporting Nantah since its inception slightly over a
decade ago, he graciously accepted the post of Chairman of the
Council on 24 May 1966. He was unanimously voted to continue his good work as Chairman in the elections for the Council

---

[viii]*Nantah School News*, Vol 1, No. 22, September 1969.

in 1968, and had held this position till 1970, when he was succeeded by Wee Cho Yaw (黄祖耀).

Founding of Nantah

Siak Kew's involvement with the first university in Southeast Asia which catered to the graduates of Chinese high schools dated back to the period of its difficult birth. The idea was first mooted by Tan Lark Sye, at a meeting at the Hokkien Clan Association on 16 January 1953. As a close associate, and a fervent advocate for higher education, Siak Kew was on board right from the beginning, officially leading the Chinese Chamber of Commerce in expressing support for this proposal five days later, on 21 January. The Singapore Chinese Chamber of Commerce also brought up this proposal at the 6th meeting of representatives from the Associated Chinese Chambers of Commerce of Malaya (马华商联会第六届代表大会).

In addition to Siak Kew's personal education experiences and support for Chinese education, his advocacy for a Chinese-language university also tied in with his fervent support for citizenship, examined in the previous chapters. In January 1953, he publicly stated:

> 目前居住本地的华人，大多数已认本地为家乡，在本地创办一间大学培育子弟，为本地服务，实为一件有意义的工作…中国南洋交通既断，吾人要生活于斯，建一大学乃属必要，吾人应广大范围组织起来，使新马各界华人团结而为，事当不难成功，新马二三百万华人，读华文者实多余读英文，有一间大学始能造成人才，始能有出路。[89]

There are many Chinese who now live here and consider Singapore their home. Therefore, it is a meaningful task to set up a university to nurture youth to serve their home ... Since China has cut off transport networks with Nanyang, and Chinese now settle here, the establishment of a university is a necessity. With proper organisation and cooperation between Chinese in Malaya and Singapore, this is not a difficult task. There are two to three million Chinese in Malaya and Singapore, and more Chinese-educated than English-educated, so a university which caters to this talent, will definitely be a success.

As with his comments on the citizenship issue, Siak Kew was keenly aware of the suspicions the British colonial government bore towards the Chinese in Singapore and the fears that their loyalty lay elsewhere. Hence, his deliberate emphasis on the situation that Chinese have settled here, especially now that China has cut off communication and transport networks.

Unfortunately, this was insufficient to allay the fears of the colonial government. These fears sometimes seemed to be on radically opposite ends of a political spectrum, with the *Malayan Political Intelligence Report of 1953* raising the concern that the foundation of the university was an extension of Kuomintang's foreign policy, compared with a 1954 Report that claimed the 'Nan Yang University might to a greater or lesser degree come under Communist influence.'[90] Nevertheless, the bottom-line was that the colonial government thought it was externally motivated rather than a truly local movement.

The founding of Nantah was plagued with further opposition from the English-language press, which questioned the need for a second university when the University of Malaya, founded in 1949, had yet to reach its full potential. As historians Lee Guan Kin and Zhou Zhao Cheng argue, these commentators 'spared no effort in defending the English-language education, for they were indifferent to China and the Chinese language.'[91] This was also the stance taken publicly by the colonial government, when dealing with the proponents of the university. In February 1953, Siak Kew was part of a delegation — which included Tan Lark Sye, Lee Kong Chian, Ng Aik Huan, and Tan Cheng Lock — to meet with Malcolm MacDonald, then Chancellor of the University of Malaya and

Commissioner-General for the United Kingdom in Southeast Asia to discuss the issue. At this meeting, Tan Lark Sye dismissed MacDonald's suggestion to them to bide their time, and wait for the University of Malaya to set up a Chinese Studies Department.[92] Contrasted with the Chinese Chamber of Commerce's earlier unconditional support for the University of Malaya, donating $500,000, of which a fifth was contributed by Siak Kew,[93] the opposition from the English-speaking public must have been a great disappointment.

Undeterred, the Chinese business community pressed ahead with their plans. By 20 February, they had decided on the name Nanyang University, reflecting their ideals for a Chinese-language university which still emphasised the importance of localisation. The Nanyang University Private Limited was registered on 5 May and a flurry of fund-raising activities began and lasted till the following year. On 26 July, Tan Lark Sye officiated the groundbreaking ceremony on the site in Jurong, donated by the Hokkien Huay Kuan.

Figure 18. Nanyang University Planning Committee. Siak Kew is fourth from left, standing to the right of Tan Lark Sye.
Source: Hu Xingrong, *Remembering Nantah* (Guilin: Guangxi Shitan University Press, 2006) [胡兴荣. 记忆南洋大学 (桂林：广西师范大学出版社, 2006)].

While it was not surprising that prominent businessmen formed the bulk of the list of contributors and donors, with Siak Kew donating $100,000 under the name of his company, Buan Lee Seng, what was truly heartening to the fundraising committee were the donations which poured in from people of working-class backgrounds, including associations of trishaw riders and taxi drivers.[94] Prominent leaders from the Indian Chamber of Commerce, including Hardial Singh, Makhanlull Mahawar, Balwant Singh, and W. Hassaram also joined the fund-raising efforts of Nantah in the following year.[95] This was turning out to be a truly people's university.

Despite their reservations, the colonial government gradually came round to the establishment of Nantah. At a meeting in January 1954, Siak Kew, together with Ko Teck Kin and Lim Kim Chuan,

Figure 19. Meeting with William Goode in January 1954, attended by Lim Kim Chuan, Ng Ai Huan, Siak Kew, and Tan Lark Sye (clockwise from left foreground). *Source*: Courtesy of National Archives of Singapore, Ministry of Information and the Arts collection.

led by Tan Lark Sye, managed to secure Colonial Secretary William Goode's assurance that donations made to Nantah will be tax-exempt. The committee continued to find opportunities to allay the colonial government's fears, such as hosting a dinner in Padang and inviting the delegates from the 2nd World Assembly of Youth, and using it as a platform to announce internationally that Nantah is apolitical and will not limit either its language of instruction or student intake to Chinese.[96]

Colony to Self-Government: Suspicions Remain

After their initial jubilance, the Lin Yutang incident threatened to derail the efforts of the many involved. While the appointment of Lin Yutang, noted bilingual scholar, as Chancellor of Nantah in 1954 was a triumph, his departure in 1955, together with 12 faculty members, was a severe embarrassment to the committee. It began with a surprisingly large budget for the University drafted by Lin in January 1955, which seemed unreasonable to the expenditure committee. As one of the Treasurers of the Council, Siak Kew was present at several of the futile meetings to resolve this dispute in February,[97] and ultimately Lin resigned in April.[98] Upon leaving, Lin's allegations that his departure was a result of his anti-communist stance further biased public opinion against the fledging university, which officially began classes in January 1956.

The government continued its policy of wary tolerance, allowing it to function as a university but without giving it due recognition, promising neither state funding nor recognition of its degrees in the civil service. With the mass involvement of Chinese students in allegedly communist protests in the 1950s, the Labour Front government inherited the colonial administrators' suspicion of Nantah. The future plans for merger with Malaya also made Nantah's is only recently we have been trying to send students to the universities abroad to get their diplomas.

2.33 p.m.

Mr. William Tan: Mr. Speaker, Sir, the policy of the Government is to provide equal treatment for all schools. Why cannot the Minister for Education accord to Nanyang University the same treatment as is given to the University of Malaya? As we all know, Nanyang University came into being through the efforts of certain rich merchants and a very big number of workers of all types, who, because they had the interest of Chinese education of this country at heart, voluntarily devoted their time and money in building Nanyang University in 1954.

Nanyang University, established this year, will provide further studies for those students leaving Chinese schools after they have passed Senior Middle School examinations. I cannot understand why Government should delay the recognition of degrees from Nanyang University. The University should deserve the fullest support from Government.

I would also remind the Minister for Education that 60 per cent of the students at present studying in Nanyang University are from the Federation. The Government should therefore make an attempt to try and get financial support from the Federation Government. If you look at the two Bills—one for the University of Malaya and the other for Nanyang University—you will see that there is discrimination. Why should there be discrimination? Even the Nanyang University Students' Union, a very important organ of the University, has been left out of the Nanyang University Bill. Is not this discrimination? Government, instead of showing equal treatment for all the students of Singapore, is thinking of barring the students from forming their union. The Minister for Education just said that he will amend that clause. The students' body of the University of Malaya also raise their objection to this omission. I think it is the concern of Government that Nanyang University should be put

under its wing, and grant-in-aid extended to it.

2.37 p.m.

Mr. Tan Siak Kew (Nominated): Mr. Speaker, Sir, as one of the eleven original founders of Nanyang University, I thought I ought to rise, not only to support the Government, but to thank it for bringing this Bill to the Assembly. I might perhaps also try to clarify some of the misunderstandings about Nanyang University.

Nanyang University was proposed at a time when the founders were convinced that, because the student population in the Chinese schools was very much bigger than that in the English schools, they had a need to go out for higher studies. That need was not available here, in view of the state that the University of Malaya was in. They could not accept enough students so as to prevent them from being attracted to China and other overseas territories for their higher education.

At the start, a lot of misunderstanding was created and there was strong opposition to the establishment of this University, because it was thought that the founding of Nanyang University would divert private donations from the University of Malaya; and secondly, it might create a divergence of loyalty. The founders were convinced that they would be helping the country by helping to absorb these surplus students for their higher education. I hope it is now fully proved that not only does it not divert the common loyalty, but it is also now taking in students whom the University of Malaya cannot take, students in fact from English schools.

The common misunderstanding about Nanyang University is perhaps this—as a Member has just mentioned—that it is only for Chinese education. In fact, it is not. Any student of Nanyang University must know English. In fact, a lot of the subjects in the faculties have to be taught in English—Science, Commerce and so on—so that, in fact, it is at least a bilingual university.

[MR. TAN SIAK KEW.]

It was due to the unity of purpose of the founders and the people that we have been able to create Nanyang University. Last year, Sir, professors from the United Kingdom who came over here and paid a visit to the University had variously estimated the buildings, hostels, the library, including the three faculties, to cost round about $25 million when we had actually spent about $6.8 million. I am still one of the Treasurers of the University, and we know that the cost of this University would, in fact, be less than that of the Polytechnic which the Government is building. Now that is one of the misunderstandings which I want to remove. It is not only a university for Chinese learning. In fact, we already have plans to teach Malay. All students, whether they be Malay, Indian, or even European would be equally welcome into the University. We hope also that if this misunderstanding is removed, the Government of the Federation of Malaya will realise, as the Singapore Government, I think has fully realised now, that it is in fact an undertaking on the same national basis as the University of Malaya, and will give it more support.

Quite recently, we had to debate whether an increase in fees should be introduced next year. The fees at the start were $30. The original students still pay $30, but for the students who joined last year, they will have to pay $60. For next year it has been proposed that this fee, in order to cover the necessary expenditure, should be increased to $100 per pupil. It is quite understandable that with the present trade recession the merchants who had originally undertaken to contribute very large sums are perhaps finding difficulty in doing so now, and the Government of Singapore must be prepared to support Nanyang University to a very much larger extent if it is to be kept going as it is now. I also hope the Federation Government will fully understand the purposes of the University, and in time also give their support to it, since it has been pointed out that over 60 per cent of the students in Nanyang University are from the Federation.

2.45 p.m.

The Minister for Local Government, Lands and Housing (Dato Abdul Hamid bin Haji Jumat): Mr. Speaker, Sir, I was somewhat disturbed to hear the speech of the Member for Changi (Mr. Lim Cher Kheng) this morning. I do not know why he has particularly singled out the Malays in connection with the Nanyang University Bill which was introduced by the Minister for Education.

Mr. Lim Cher Kheng: For a good reason.

Dato Abdul Hamid: To my mind, Sir, I think that this is a dangerous and deliberate attempt to foster communalism in this Assembly. What I want to know, Sir, from the Member for Changi is this. Is he insinuating that we, the Malays of Singapore, are anti-Nanyang University? Is he trying to say that we, the Malays of Singapore, are anti-Chinese culture?

Mr. Lim Cher Kheng: I never said that.

Mr. Speaker: Order.

Dato Abdul Hamid: If he is, Sir, then he is making a very great mistake.

Mr. Lim Cher Kheng rose ——

Mr. Speaker: Is it on a point of elucidation?

Mr. Lim Cher Kheng: On a point of explanation, Sir.

Mr. Speaker: If the Minister will give way.

Dato Abdul Hamid: I will not give way.

Mr. Lim Cher Kheng: Coward!

Mr. Speaker: Order. The hon. Member knows that that word is not permitted in this Assembly. Will he please withdraw that word?

Figure 20. Extracts from Singapore Legislative Assembly Debates.

Source: Official Report of the Third Session of the First Legislative Assembly Debates, First Series, Volume 8, Part III of Session 1958.

position tenuous, as there was no certainty how the Federation government will look upon the existence of a university which had no Federal counterpart.

In one of a series of crackdowns on suspected communist elements in 1958, Chief Minister Lim Yew Hock dealt a blow to Nantah by revoking the citizenship of its Registrar, Pan Kuo Chu.[99] However, possibly due to impending elections in 1959, Lim Yew Hock seized the opportunity to table the Nanyang University Bill in November 1958 in order to win the votes of the Chinese majority. The Bill did not promise immediate recognition, as that would have to wait for a formal assessment to be conducted the following year. The Bill, however, did provide for a new university council of twenty-eight members, of which three would be government nominees, and could be interpreted as an olive branch and the beginning of the slow process towards government recognition of Nantah.

The impending elections made the Bill a popular one in the Assembly. Historian Edwin Lee even goes as far as to suggest that 'it was the anticipation of the power of the overwhelmingly Chinese electorate that had brought legislators to such unanimity' when debating the Bill. It was no simple feat considering the Assembly then comprised of five parties, independent members and nominated members; all voicing out their approval of the Nanyang University Bill. Amidst the jostling for political points in the Second Reading of the Nanyang University Bill on 3 December 1958, Siak Kew spoke up on the issue as an impartial nominated member of the Assembly. In a systematic and detailed manner, he clarified the common misconception that Nantah only catered to Chinese by dispelling the common misconceptions and appealing for government support.

If the Assembly's approval of the Bill gave Nantah a glimmer of hope, the S. L. Prescott assessment in January 1959 and the follow up review by Gwee Ah Leng later that year were to disappoint well-wishers of Nantah yet again. Both did not recommend government recognition of Nantah graduates. The change in government, with a landslide victory by the People's Action Party (PAP) with 43 out of 51 seats in May 1959, did not affect the attitudes towards Nantah. In fact, the PAP government began to suggest a reorganisation of Nantah, much to the ire of Tan Lark Sye. The Nantah Liaison Committee talks to negotiate what to reform began in 1960 to a rocky start

Figure 21. Negotiations between representatives of the Singapore government and the Nantah Council in 1963. From top right corner in an anti-clockwise direction: Ko Teck Kin, Siak Kew, Lau Geok Swee, Ng Aik Huan, Jek Yuen Thong, Lee Khoon Choy, and Tan Kee Gak.
Source: Straits Times © Singapore Press Holdings Ltd. Reprinted with permission.

and was suspended for three years. Tan Lark Sye began to challenge the PAP government openly, first by installing Chuang Chu Lin, a known leftist, as Vice-Chancellor of Nantah, and the final straw came when he publicly urged the Hokkien Huay Kuan to support the Barisan Socialis in the September 1963 general elections. Tan's citizenship was later removed in 1964, thus removing a thorn in their sides.[100]

These series of events necessitated a less confrontational approach and a return to the negotiation table. Led by the Nantah

Figure 22.   Taking a break from the intensive negotiations on the issue of recognition of Nantah's degrees in 1963. From left to right: Jek Yuen Thong, Siak Kew, Lee Khoon Choy, and Tan Kee Gak.
Source: Straits Times © Singapore Press Holdings Ltd. Reprinted with permission.

Council's Vice-Chairman, Lau Geok Swee, Siak Kew — together with Ko Teck Kin (Nantah Council's Treasurer), Ng Aik Huan, and Tan Kee Gak — met with government representatives, Lee Khoon Choy (Parliamentary Secretary to the Ministry of Education) and Jek Yuen Thong (Political Secretary to the Prime Minister).[101] These negotiations were to go on intermittently until an agreement was hammered out by mid-1964, with Chuang's resignation and the formation of a new Nanyang University Council, helmed by Ko Teck Kin, in exchange for the possibility of recognising Nantah degrees in the future.[102]

Separation: More Turbulence for Nantah

The shock of the political separation from the Federation of Malaysia barely wore off when Nantah students were to experience yet another blow from the Wang Gungwu Report made public a month later in September 1965. Students took offence at yet another undermining of Nantah's curriculum, degree structure, and medium of instruction, fearing that it threatened to displace the Chinese language. These protests continued till November.[103] Once again, Siak Kew, together with Ko Teck Kin and Ng Aik Huan, found himself occupying the unenviable position as a mediator between the government and an angry student populace. They managed to get Prime Minister Lee Kuan Yew's assurance that the spirit of their former agreement still holds and Chinese language will still continue to be the medium of instruction. In exchange, the 85 students expelled for their protests against the Wang Gungwu Report were offered a chance for re-instatement.[104]

Tragedy was to strike again with Ko Teck Kin's unexpected death in April 1966. Siak Kew was a natural successor, given his involvement in former discussions with the government and first-hand knowledge of what was necessary to protect Nantah's fragile status.

Figure 23.   Siak Kew, as Chairman of University Council, accompanies guest-of-honour, President Yusof Ishak, for the Nanyang University's Convocation Ceremony on 20 May 1967.
Source: Courtesy of National Archives of Singapore, Yusof Ishak Collection.

He continued to hold this position till 1970, when he was succeeded by Wee Cho Yaw.

During his tenure as Council Chairman, in 1968, Nantah finally obtained what it had fought for since its foundation: the official recognition of its degrees by the government. Other developments Siak Kew oversaw included the introduction of Malay Studies Department (1968), the hiring of Professor Rayson Huang (黄丽松) as the Vice-Chancellor (1969), and the setting up of the Nantah Development Foundation (南大发展基金), which Siak Kew had led by example with a personal donation of $100,000 in 1967.

Under his leadership, Nantah reformed along the lines as required by the government but without losing its founding mission: that of providing a uniquely localised variant of Chinese

Figure 24. Siak Kew delivering a convocation speech as University Council Chairman, undated.
Source: Image courtesy of Mr Tan Puay Hiang.

tertiary education. Unfortunately, this dream came before its time. While politicians today urge Singaporeans to embrace bilingualism and a deeper study of Chinese language and culture in a bid to tap on the rising economic success of China, the 1950s and 1960s were a very different time and Nantah's birth was plagued by the spectre of communalism and contesting views of nationhood. Siak Kew's dream for the university, regrettably, could not be sustained as it was merged with the University of Singapore to form the National University of Singapore in 1980.

Diplomat by Duty

After all, the chain of command is identical whether in the foreign
service or in the field of business and finance. Both worlds operate
through executives. I shall keep in mind the overall picture and let the
senior staff get on with the day-to-day details.

— *Tan Siak Kew, when interviewed in May 1966 upon being appointed
Ambassador of Thailand*[ix]

[ix] "When a Merchant Banker turns Diplomat," *The Straits Times*, 1 May 1966, p. 8.

W hen Siak Kew was appointed Ambassador to Thailand in 1966, a staff reporter from *The Straits Times* wrote an appropriately glowing profile of the man, describing the 63-year-old as 'a scholar by inclination, a businessman by necessity, and now a diplomat through a sense of duty.'[105] Siak Kew's contributions to Singapore in the political, social, and commercial spheres have been outlined in the previous chapters, and now we turn to his role as a diplomat by duty.

Gentleman Adviser

Before his appointment as Ambassador to Thailand in 1966, Siak Kew had already represented Singapore countless times in

Figure 25.   Representing Singapore, Siak Kew also participated in trade missions abroad with the Chinese Chamber of Commerce, such as the 1958 trade mission to Australia and New Zealand in October 1958, to examine ways to expand the trading networks in Singapore.
Source: Image courtesy of Mr Tan Puay Hiang.

Figure 26. In Melbourne, they paid a visit to the plant of the International Harvester Company at Geelong, 45 miles from Melbourne, examining the factory of the company which exported tractors, harvesters, and other agricultural machines to Asian countries.
Source: Image courtesy of Mr Tan Puay Hiang.

international contexts. As a Chinese Chamber of Commerce member, he participated in numerous trade missions. In 1961, he was also the sole representative from Singapore to attend the International Industrial Conference in San Francisco.[106] Over 500 trade, industrial, financial, and development organisation leaders from the United States, Europe, and Asia attended this International Industrial Conference which discussed the issues facing the world economy in the decade to come and the roles private enterprises may play to face these challenges.[107]

As a prominent business leader, and nominated member of the Legislative Assembly, as well as the Chairman of the Trade Advisory Board, Siak Kew's many hats lent weight to his views at such regional and international forums. The fact that he was effectively bilingual and his balanced demeanour did not hurt either. In fact, he left a lasting impression on a young civil servant during a trip to the 1958 Economic Commission for Asia and the Far East (ECAFE) Conference in Bangkok. The ECAFE was then the premier regional economic organisation of the area, allowing members to discuss development and trade in the region. This young civil servant was none other than Professor Lim Chong Yah, eminent economist and the first Chairman of the National Wages Council in 1972.

Accompanied by O. H. R. Beadles, Deputy Secretary of the Ministry for Commerce and Industry, and the 26-year-old Lim Chong Yah, Siak Kew went along as an Adviser, because of his business connections with the Thais. Indeed, the two civil servants were in awe of the treatment they received because of the companionship, with Lim recalling how that was the first time he had sat in an air-conditioned chauffer-driven car. They were put up in Erawan Hotel, which Lim had felt was a 'seven-star hotel' then.

It was not all about material comfort. Siak Kew also brought Beadles and Lim around Bangkok, not only to the scenic spots such as the Botanic Gardens, but more importantly, introducing them to the various movers and shakers in the headquarters of ECAFE. Lim especially recalls meeting Dr Puey Ungphakorn, the Governor of the Central Bank, who was Siak Kew's friend. Two decades later, Lim would speak, in the capacity as an academic at the University of Singapore, during the conferment of an honorary doctorate from the National University of Singapore on this economist whom he had met in the trip with Siak Kew.[108]

Siak Kew was also a gentleman to the young Lim, behaving like a pseudo-mentor to the young civil servant who was so enamoured with the vast difference between Singapore and the metropolis that was Bangkok then. During mealtimes and their journeys between meetings, they spoke about society, education, the changing world order, and the disparity between Singapore and Bangkok. Siak Kew's actions also impressed Lim, who admired his disciplined demeanour, insisting on keeping to his habit of retiring at 8 pm every night to cool down and to ensure he had sufficient rest for the next day.

Siak Kew even went as far as to read through Lim's speech, which he had drafted for his superior, Beadles. Lim fondly recounts how Siak Kew was a supportive adviser:

> We had participated as a colony. My head [Beadles] was supposed to deliver a paper and I wrote a speech for him. Mr Tan was very happy with the speech, but my boss said, 'We are a small place, we are a colony. It's very difficult for me to go and propound global solutions. That is a little out of my reach. It's not for me to go and suggest ways and means to have a better world, a more rational global environment.' I was completely out-of-tune! In a way — though he didn't say it — (he meant to say) "Your speech is too provocative." But Mr Tan was more sympathetic. I think, to young people like me, his attitude was to give them as much room as possible. And that brought us closer to each other.

Though it is not known exactly what this provocative speech that Lim had drafted entailed, Beadles ultimately did not make any comments on the global economy. He ended up delivering a rather mild pledge that Singapore and British Borneo will continue their policies of free and liberal trading with minimum controls and outlined the policies the colony will take to improve the port facilities to maintain the volume of trade.[109]

Nor did this supportive attitude end with the short ECAFE mission. Lim recollects that when he returned from his PhD from University of Oxford and his teaching stint at University of Malaya in the late 1960s, Siak Kew was one of the first few people he contacted in Singapore. Hosting a lunch for the academic, Siak Kew did not beat around the bush when he asked bluntly, "Why did you come back? Do you have relatives in top places in Singapore?" Lim was so shocked and surprised by the questions that he still remembers it vividly today. Though we will never know why Siak Kew had asked these questions, one thing is certain — that he had been following Lim's career and meteoric rise in academia and in the Kuala Lumpur branch of the University of Malaya. That was probably why he was so curious of why Lim had chosen to return to Singapore, that he dispensed with the niceties of welcoming his friend, but asked directly why he chose to return.

Pioneer Ambassador

Lim commented that Siak Kew was a 'first rate choice' for the Ambassador to Thailand, which had found itself in need of one when it unexpectedly became independent on 9 August 1965. Thailand recognised Singapore on 14 August 1965, and accordingly upgraded its existing consulate general to an embassy. There was also probably a practical reason for appointing Siak Kew as the Ambassador to Thailand. As a Teochew community leader in Singapore, Siak Kew's standing among the Thai business community was well-established even in the 1950s.

For all his business networks and connections, Siak Kew was not what the Thais had expected. As his successor, Ho Rih Hwa, mentioned in his memoirs, there were rumours that some members of the Thai government had not been too welcoming of men from the mercantile classes assuming diplomatic positions due to a clause in the 1815 treaty which stated that diplomats must be men of noble birth or high rank in the government.[110] It was fortunate that the Foreign Minister S. Rajaratnam did not let these reservations stemming from some archaic agreement between European nations dictate the choice of Ambassador, or Singapore would have lost an ideal pioneer Ambassador to Thailand.

Upon accepting the appointment as Ambassador, Siak Kew wrote to Rajaratnam in February 1966, expressing his concerns:

Figure 27   Siak Kew presenting his credentials to Her Royal Highness the Princess Mother on 2 September 1966, in the absence of King Bhumibol.
Source: Image courtesy of Mr Tan Puay Hiang.

'I may not be what you might call a career or professional diplomat. I am not familiar with formalities of protocols and I shall need strong capable support.' He further added that he did not intend to 'benefit by any pecuniary gain from the appointment and I shall only be trying to do the job out of a sense of public duty and as a grateful gesture to government which has entrusted me, an amateur, with this appointment.'[111] Characteristically humble, Siak Kew was aware that he was not the typical diplomat, but nevertheless took the task on as his patriotic duty.

Siak Kew's unorthodox and non-diplomatic ways, ironically, made him a good choice for the role. As recounted by S. R. Nathan, then Assistant Secretary in Ministry of Foreign Affairs, Singapore-Thai

Figure 28.   When Siak Kew arrived in Thailand, the who's who in Thailand's business community turned up to present a garland and welcome him. Among those in attendance were Udane Tejapaibul (first row, second from left), Chairman of Bangkok Metropolitan Bank and owner of Thailand's second largest brewery, and U Chu Liang (first row, third from right), Chairman of Bara Windsor, a major motor car assembly and distributor firm.
Source: Image courtesy of Mr Tan Puay Hiang.

relations had gotten off to a slightly rocky start with certain prominent Singapore leaders being disparaging of Thailand's close relationship with the United States. It was not until the Prime Minister's visit in 1973 that relations became notably 'warm and constructive'.[112] Nevertheless, Siak Kew's refreshingly frank demeanour and his engaging personality clearly lent to his likeability, and the Thais were ready to overlook the comments made in a different context. In fact, the Thai government became so warm towards Siak Kew that not only their Foreign Minister, but also their Prime Minister, attended Singapore's third National Day reception hosted by Siak Kew at the Chiengmai Room of the Rama Hotel.[113]

Figure 29.   Siak Kew seen photographed here with the Thai Prime Minister Thanom Kittikachorn (extreme right), Foreign Minister Thanat Khoman (second from right), and Iranian Ambassador Dr Manoutchehr Mazban at Singapore's National Day reception in Bangkok in August 1967.
Source: Image courtesy of Mr Tan Puay Hiang.

Despite the goodwill Siak Kew received from the Thais, he had his work cut out for him. Operating out of a room in the Viengtai Hotel and later a suite in the Rama Hotel, the first task on the Ambassador's plate was to secure a more permanent arrangement. While Siak Kew had identified the former Italian Ambassador's residence, which was a 'substantially built house' at No. 90 North Sathorn Road 'with broad frontage and lawn' and 'of the old type architecture, quite impressive looking from the roadside', it was not till March 1967 that the mission was finally open. The reasons for the three-month delay were never made publicly known. Nevertheless, Siak Kew wrote back on 20 March: 'Nearly everyone I met has praised the spaciousness and style and convenience of our embassy and I am indeed happy that we should be lucky enough to get this place at North Sathorn.'[114]

Figure 30. Siak Kew making a speech at Singapore's National Day reception in August 1967.
Source: Image courtesy of Mr Tan Puay Hiang.

In addition to finding a location for the chancery, Siak Kew had to also grapple with civil bureaucratic woes. As S. R. Nathan recounts in his memoirs, a 'running feud' between the Ministry of Foreign Affairs and a permanent secretary at the Treasury meant that funds required for equipment and services for overseas missions were regulated 'to the point of absurdity'. Siak Kew's newly established Bangkok chancery was not spared. The Treasury turned down the request to hire a gardener for $30 a month, insisting that they should engage part-time gardeners as they do in London; an unfair comparison considering that the greenery required perennial attention in tropical places like Bangkok. Siak Kew was also instructed to buy made-in-Singapore furniture instead of Thai teak furniture. He complied, but the furniture from Diethelm Singapore developed cracks shortly after its arrival in Bangkok![115]

Faced with such challenges, the easiest way out for Siak Kew was to purchase his own furniture. As Lim mentions in his interview:

> At that time, our government was so poor, so hard-up, and had no money to furnish the embassy. So Mr Tan willingly furnished the entire embassy and never asked a cent back. I'm not so sure whether the government would pay, but he never asked. He thought that it was his duty. I used to laugh at it, but that was our starting point in building a nation. We needed people with that kind of attitude, that kind of mindset, to help build a country which became independent suddenly.

Siak Kew, like his successor and many other businessmen-turned-ambassadors of the period, chose to forgo the salary of $10,000 to $14,000 for the sake of patriotic duty.[116]

***

Even a short trip to Bangkok in 1958 can leave a lasting impression on a man decades down the road. The personal touch of a gentlemanly adviser at an ECAFE conference was what Lim Chong Yah remembers fondly. At the conclusion of the interview with Lim, he comments wryly, 'we are fortunate to have him as one of our early pioneers.' Indeed, as a pioneer Ambassador, he was effective and gracious to overlook the limitations placed upon him.

Conclusion

As one of the pioneers of post-independent Singapore, Siak Kew was a man who embodied a perseverant spirit towards excellence, a man who held his convictions and pursued his ideals without being dogmatic and intractable, a man who was both scholarly and pragmatic. Concious of his responsibility to the new nation to be born, Siak Kew strove to bridge the Chinese-speaking and English-speaking communities with his gift of bilingualism. He sat on the Boards of the Singapore Harbour Board, the Singapore Telephone Board, the Pineapples and Rubber Appeal Boards, and chaired the Schools Appeal Board and the Singapore Produce Exchange,[117] with his tact and non-partisan political stance. The lack of mention of his contributions to these other public bodies in the preceding discussion is not a reflection of their importance, but because there was a pressing need to limit the scope of what is essentially an introductory sketch to the man.

Beyond the veil of public service, his private life was as multifaceted as his public persona. He was a skilled calligrapher, an amateur *erhu* player, and a keen collector of ceramics. He was also a

Figure 31. At a dinner in July 1963 held in honour of Prime Minister Lee Kuan Yew (third from left) and Finance Minister Goh Keng Swee (first from right) for their success at the recent merger and Malaysia talks in London. It was hosted by the Joint Chambers of Commerce, an alliance that emphasized trade interests over racial divisions, which Siak Kew (first from left) had been heavily involved in. Over 200 prominent merchants, industrialists, and business leaders, including the President of the Indian Chamber, K. M. Abdul Razak (second from right), and President of the Chinese Chamber of Commerce, Ko Teck Kin (second from left), attended the event. Source: Straits Times © Singapore Press Holdings Ltd. Reprinted with permission.

good sportsman in his youth, being skilled at billiards, soccer, and tennis.[118] As President of the Siong Boo Athletic Association, a premier snooker and billiards club,[119] the story circulating in the sports circles was that he won the billiards championship of the club and walked away with the shield that he had donated for the

Figure 32. Siak Kew lounging on a yacht; one of the rare images of him in a leisurely state, undated.
Source: Image courtesy of Mr Tan Puay Hiang.

Figure 33. Siak Kew descending the steps from a temple in Petchaburi during one of his holidays in 1967.
Source: Image courtesy of Mr Tan Puay Hiang.

tournament. He was also an aesthete and his love and taste for Chinese antiquity was only matched by his appreciation and ownership for fine cars, some of which were products of independent makers like the Armstrong Siddely Sapphire, of which his was one of two in Southeast Asia.

Privately, he was a caring husband and father, a doting grandfather, a friend, and a mentor to many. Through the two holiday homes in Bedok and Pasir Panjang, Siak Kew provided a safe haven for his grandchildren. His generosity extended to their friends, and he had even encouraged them to use the quiet Bedok holiday home for their study during the examinations period. A dignified man at all times, Siak Kew was always formally and elegantly attired. With his strong personal discipline which was reflected by a rigid work routine and an authoritative stature, he was a charismatic and patriarchal figure who instilled discipline in his children without having to resort to the cane.

When he died at the age of 74 in 1977, members from the clans, the Chambers of Commerce, educational institutions of all levels, corporations, government bodies, and the diplomatic community paid their last respects. A senior government official remarked in admiration that the formality and breadth of the dignitaries from diverse institutions who remembered him on his passing was a testimony to the greatness of the man in life.[120] Then Prime Minister Lee Kuan Yew summed him up most aptly in his condolence message: 'He was a prominent citizen, who served his country well.'

Today, the name Tan Siak Kew lives on. Scholarships and bursaries at the National University of Singapore and Nanyang Technological University set up in his memoriam continue to bear his name.[121] Sennett Estate, the first private housing development after the Second World War built in 1951, has an avenue named after Siak Kew,[122] even if not many know of the man it was named after.

The Pingat Jasa Gemilang (Meritorious Service Medal), conferred on him for his service to the nation, was a coveted award in the late 1960s.[123]

The issues raised in this book will be relevant in future research in the transitionary era of Singapore's journey into nationhood and the men who played a part in their simple yet selfless way. It is hoped that to posterity, the name Tan Siak Kew may be recognised as one of them. He went against the grain, did what was unexpected, and left behind a legacy that is all but forgotten.

Bibliography

Periodicals and Newspapers

Berita Harian

Nantah School News [南大校讯]

The Straits Times

The Singapore Free Press and Mercantile Advertiser

Official Records

Singapore Legislative Assembly Debates

Straits Settlements Government Gazette

National Archives of Singapore

Citizenship Policy in Singapore, CO 1030/259. Microfilm Number NAB 345.

Meeting Minutes of Singapore Chinese Chamber of Commerce Committee, Vols XX to XXV, 1952 to 1959. Microfilm Number NA 008.

Oral History Interview conducted with Mr Tan Puay Hiang, by Patricia Lee in 2008. Accession Number 003353.

Academic Journals

Blackburn, Kevin. 'The Collective Memory of the Sook Ching Massacre and the Creation of the Civilian War Memorial of Singapore,' *Journal of the Malaysian Branch of the Royal Asiatic Society*, 73, 2 (2000): 71–90.

Lim, Choo Hoon. 'The Transformation of the Political Orientation of the Chinese Chamber of Commerce, 1945–1955,' *Review of Southeast Asian Studies*, 9 (1979): 1–63.

Lim, Patricia. 'Continuity and Connectedness: The Ngee Heng Kongsi of Johor, 1844–1916,' *ISEAS Visiting Researchers Series,* No. 2 (2000).

Smith, Simon C. 'Crimes and Punishment: Local Responses to the Trial of Japanese War Criminals in Malaya and Singapore, 1946–1948,' *South East Asia Research*, 5, 1 (1997): 41–56.

Trocki, Carl. 'The Johor Archives and the Kangchu System, 1844–1910,' *Journal of the Royal Asiatic Society Malaysian Branch*, 48, 1 (1975): 1–46.

Book Sources

Chew, Melanie. *Leaders of Singapore* (Singapore: Resource Press, 1996).

Chua, Ser-Koon and Hsu Yun-Tsiao (eds.). *Malayan Chinese Resistance to Japan 1937–1945: Selected Source Materials Based on Colonel Chuang Hui-Tsuan's Collection* (Singapore: Cultural & Historical Publishing House, 1984).

Ho, Rih Hwa. *Eating Salt: An Autobiography* (Singapore: Times Books International, 1991).

Hu, Xingrong. *Remembering Nantah* (Guilin: Guangxi Shifan University Press, 2006) [胡兴荣, 记忆南洋大学 (桂林: 广西师范大学出版社, 2006)].

Lee, Guan Kin (ed.). *Demarcating Ethnicity in New Nations: Cases of the Chinese in Singapore, Malaysia, and Indonesia* (Singapore: Singapore Society of Asian Studies, 2006).

Lee, Edwin. *Singapore: The Unexpected Nation* (Singapore: Institute of Southeast Asian Studies, 2008).

Lin, Wendan and Feng Qinglian. *Brief History of Singapore Clan Associations* (Singapore: Singapore Federation of Clan Associations, 2005) [林文丹＆冯清莲，*新加坡宗乡会馆史略* (新加坡：新加坡宗乡会馆联合总会, 2005)].

Liu, Gretchen. *The Singapore Foreign Service: The First 40 Years* (Singapore: Editions Didier Millet, 2005).

Nathan, S.R. and Timothy Auger. *An Unexpected Journey: Path to the Presidency* (Singapore: Editions Didier Millet, 2011).

Singapore Mandarin School Seventh Anniversary Publication (Singapore: Overseas Chinese Mandarin School, 1937) [*新加坡华侨国语学校第七周年纪念特刊* (新加坡：华侨国语学校, 1937)].

Singapore Teochew Poit Ipp Huay Kuan Golden Souvenir (Singapore: Teochew Poit Ipp Huay Kuan, 1980) [*新加坡潮州八邑会馆金禧纪念刊* (新加坡：该会馆, 1980)].

Skinner, W. G. *Report on the Chinese in Southeast Asia* (Ithaca: Cornell University, Department of Far Eastern Studies, 1950).

Song, Lusheng (ed.). *Far-East Biographies* (Singapore: Centre for Far East Biographies, 1934 & 1941) [宋鲁生, 远东人物志 (新加坡: 远东民史纂修所, 1934 & 1941)].

Song, Zhemei. *Biographies of Singapore-Malaya Personalities* (Hong Kong: Southeast Asia Research Institute, 1969) [宋哲美, *星马人物志* (香港: 东南亚研究所, 1969)].

Tan, Yeok Seong. *History of the Formation of the Oversea Chinese Association and The Extortion by J.M.A. of $50,000,000 Military Contribution from the Chinese in Malaya* (Singapore: Nanyang Book Co., 1947).

Turnbull, C. M. *A History of Modern Singapore, 1819–2005* (Singapore: NUS Press, 2009).

Visscher, Sikko. *The Business of Politics and Ethnicity: A History of the Singapore Chinese Chamber of Commerce and Industry* (Singapore: NUS Press, 2007).

Wang, Ruming. *These Fifty Years: Nantah's Fiftieth Anniversary, 1955–2005* (Singapore: Singapore Nantah Alumni, 2005) [王如明, 呵, 这五十年：*南洋大学创办五十周年纪念, 1955–2005* (新加坡: 新加坡南洋大学毕业生协会, 2005)].

Yap, Pheng Geck. *Scholar, Banker, Gentleman Soldier: The Reminiscences of Dr. Yap Pheng Geck* (Singapore: Times Books International, 1982).

Yeo, Kim Wah. *Political Development in Singapore, 1945–1955* (Singapore: Singapore University Press, 1973).

Yong, C. F. *Tan Kah-kee: The Making of An Overseas Chinese legend* (Singapore: Oxford University Press, 1987).

Endnotes

1. Taken from Mr Tan Puay Hiang's oral history interview Reel 2 003353/2.
2. "When a Merchant Banker Turns Diplomat," *The Straits Times*, 1 May 1966, p. 8.
3. Date is based on lunar calendar date — fifth day of the fifth month (五月初五) — as stated in Song Lusheng, *Far-East Biographies* (Singapore: Centre for Far East Biographies, 1934) [宋鲁生, 远东人物志 (新加坡: 远东民史纂修所, 1934)]. Much of the content within this chapter is drawn from the above source, complemented with other comments made by Siak Kew's family.
4. See for instance, Carl Trocki, 'The Johor Archives and the Kangchu System, 1844–1910,' *Journal of the Royal Asiatic Society Malaysian Branch*, 48, 1 (1975): 1–46; Patricia Lim, 'Continuity and Connectedness: The Ngee Heng Kongsi of Johor, 1844–1916', *ISEAS Visiting Researchers Series*, No. 2 (2000).
5. "When a Merchant Banker Turns Diplomat," *The Straits Times*, 1 May 1966, p. 8.
6. *Singapore Mandarin School Seventh Anniversary Publication* (Singapore: Overseas Chinese Mandarin School, 1937) [新加坡华侨国语学校第七周年纪念特刊 (新加坡: 华侨国语学校, 1937)].
7. Song Lusheng, *Far-East Biographies* (Singapore: Centre for Far East Biographies, 1934) [宋鲁生, 远东人物志 (新加坡: 远东民史纂修所, 1934)].
8. Song Zhemei (ed.), *Biographies of Singapore-Malaya Personalities* (Hong Kong: Southeast Asia Research Institute, 1969) [宋哲美(ed.), 星马人物志 (香港: 东南亚研究所, 1969)], p. 61.
9. Song Lusheng, *Far-East Biographies* (Singapore: Centre for Far East Biographies, 1941) [宋鲁生, 远东人物志 (新加坡: 远东民史纂修所, 1941)], p. 59.

10. "China Famine Fund," *The Singapore Free Press and Mercantile Advertiser*, 8 December 1920, p. 14.
11. "Salvation Army Needs Help," *The Straits Times*, 31 March 1937, p. 17.
12. "Salvation Army," *SFPMA*, 11 May 1937, p. 7.
13. "Singapore Aid for Starving Szechuan," *The Straits Times*, 17 May 1937, p. 12 .
14. Chua Ser-Koon and Hsu Yun-Tsiao (eds.), *Malayan Chinese Resistance to Japan 1937–1945: Selected Source Materials Based on Colonel Chuang Hui-Tsuan's Collection* (Singapore: Cultural & Historical Pub. House, 1984), p. 2.
15. Yap Pheng Geck also notes that the majority of the English-educated remained unconcerned with events in China until the late 1930s.
16. "Singapore Chinese's $250,000 Relief Fund One Big Gift," *The Straits Times*, 16 August 1937, p. 12.
17. Chua Ser Koon notes CNC$3 million was raised by 19 December 1937, and at an exchange rate of Straits $51.50 to CNC$100, that amounted to about $1,545,000.
18. Chua and Hsu, *Malayan Chinese Resistance to Japan*, p. 5.
19. "Malayan War Charity Fund Opened Today," *The Straits Times*, 7 September 1939, p. 10.
20. "Chinese Donations to War Fund Now Total $67,575," *The Straits Times*, 26 September 1939, p. 11.
21. "More Chinese Gifts to the Patriotic Fund," *The Straits Times*, 22 December 1939, p. 13.
22. "Today's Donations," *The Straits Times*, 4 June 1940, p. 10; "Chinese Gesture in Poppy Day Gifts," *SFPMA*, 5 November 1940, p. 7.
23. Straits Settlements Government Gazette No. 1110, CO276/159.
24. "Editorial: Folly," *The Straits Times*, 4 February 1941, p. 8.
25. "Mr Tay Lian Teck and Income Tax," *The Straits Times*, 3 February 1941, p. 12.
26. Chua and Hsu, *Malayan Chinese Resistance to Japan*, pp. 35–36.
27. The statistics of those who perished in Sook Ching ranged between 5000, as claimed by the Japanese during the war crimes trial, and 50,000, as claimed by local Chinese reports.
28. Yap Pheng Geck, *Scholar, Banker, Gentleman Soldier: The Reminiscences of Dr. Yap Pheng Geck* (Singapore: Times Books International, 1982), p. 56.

29. Melanie Chew, *Leaders of Singapore* (Singapore: Resource Press, 1996), p. 43.

30. Chew, *Leaders of Singapore*, p. 41.

31. Chua and Hsu, *Malayan Chinese Resistance to Japan*, p. 379.

32. Chua and Hsu, *Malayan Chinese Resistance to Japan*, pp. 380 and 381.

33. Tan Y. S., *History of the Formation of the Oversea Chinese Association and the Extortion by J.M.A. of $50,000,000 Military Contribution from the Chinese in Malaya* (Singapore: Nanyang Book Co., 1947), p. 3.

34. Chua and Hsu, *Malayan Chinese Resistance to Japan*, p. 39.

35. *Ibid.*

36. The last meeting he had attended, according to the meeting minutes reproduced in Chua and Hsu, pp. 376–397, was on 13 June 1942.

37. Chew, *Leaders of Singapore*, p. 43.

38. Information provided by Mr Tan Puay Hiang.

39. Simon C. Smith, 'Crimes and Punishment: Local Responses to the Trial of Japanese War Criminals in Malaya and Singapore, 1946–1948,' *South East Asia Research*, 5, 1 (1997): 46–52.

40. Kevin Blackburn, 'The Collective Memory of the Sook Ching Massacre and the Creation of the Civilian War Memorial of Singapore,' *Journal of the Malaysian Branch of the Royal Asiatic Society*, 73, 2 (2000): 71–90.

41. W. G. Skinner, *Report on the Chinese in Southeast Asia* (Ithaca: Cornell University Department of Far Eastern Studies, 1950), p. 32.

42. Sikko Visscher, *The Business of Politics and Ethnicity: A History of the Singapore Chinese Chamber of Commerce and Industry* (Singapore: NUS Press, 2007), p. 80.

43. Lim Choo Hoon, 'The Transformation of the Political Orientation of the Chinese Chamber of Commerce, 1945–1955,' *Review of Southeast Asian Studies*, 9 (1979): 35.

44. "'Give Franchise to China-Born Chinese in Singapore' Plea," *The Straits Times*, 6 January 1951, p. 5.

45. Lim, 'The Transformation of the Political Orientation of the Chinese Chamber of Commerce, 1945–1955,' p. 36.

46. Colonial Secretary to Singapore Chinese Chambers of Commerce, 22/2/1952, cited in Yeo Kim Wah, *Political Development in Singapore, 1945–55* (Singapore: Singapore University Press, 1973), op. cit. p. 145.

47. "Chinese Citizens," *The Straits Times*, 20 December 1951, p. 8.

48. Singapore Chinese Chamber of Commerce Meeting Minutes [hereafter SCCC meeting minutes], 29 August 1952. National Archives of Singapore, NA008.

49. Lim, 'The Transformation of the Political Orientation of the Chinese Chamber of Commerce, 1945–1955,' p. 38.

50. *Ibid.*, pp. 38–39.

51. Visscher, *The Business of Politics and Ethnicity*, pp. 106–107.

52. "Citizenship for the Lost Thousands," *The Straits Times*, 19 August 1955, p. 5.

53. Memorandum for the Information of the Secretary of State, 10 August 1955. CO 1030/259.

54. Singapore Legislative Assembly Debates, Third Session of the First Legislative Assembly, First Series, Vol 6, Part 1 of Session 1958, 23 April 1958, col 164.

55. Lin Wendan and Feng Qinglian, *Brief History of Singapore Clan Associations* (Singapore: Singapore Federation of Associations, 2005) [林文丹 & 冯清莲, 新加坡宗乡会馆史略 (新加坡: 新加坡宗乡会馆联合总会, 2005)], pp. 199–202.

56. *Ibid.*

57. *Singapore Teochew Poit Ipp Huay Kuan Golden Souvenir* (Singapore: Teochew Poit Ipp Huay Kuan, 1980) [新加坡潮州八邑会馆金禧纪念刊 (新加坡: 该会馆, 1980)], p. 64.

58. "Policy Rift Halts Ngee Ann College Extension," *The Straits Times*, 27 May 1965, p. 6.

59. "The Ngee Ann College Crisis is Over," *The Straits Times*, 9 June 1965, p. 11.

60. "No Cash, but College Will Keep Honours," *The Straits Times*, 10 June 1965, p. 6.

61. "Extension Work at Ngee Ann to Go On," *The Straits Times*, 24 June 1965, p. 5.

62. "Dialect Bias Seen at a Wedding," *The Straits Times*, 17 August 1987, p. 15.

63. Visscher, *The Business of Politics and Ethnicity*, p. 92.

64. *Ibid.*

65. Tan Kah Kee was initially pro-nationalist, but after the war, he eventually began to throw his weight behind the Chinese Communist Party. He eventually left Singapore in 1949, was denied re-entry into Malaya in 1950,

and settled down in China, serving numerous positions in the Communist Party before his death in Beijing in 1961. See C. F. Yong, *Tan Kah-kee: The Making of an Overseas Chinese Legend* (Singapore: Oxford University Press, 1987).

66. "Thirteen Members Resign," *The Straits Times*, 3 October 1946, p. 5.

67. "Resignations Withdrawn," *The Straits Times*, 5 October 1946, p. 3.

68. SCCC meeting minutes, 29 January 1951.

69. SCCC meeting minutes, 17 June 1952.

70. "'Not Too Far, but Too Fast' — Taylor," *The Straits Times*, 26 February 1954, p. 7.

71. SCCC meeting minutes, 26 March 1954.

72. Visscher, *The Business of Politics and Ethnicity*, p. 104.

73. C. M. Turnbull, *A History of Modern Singapore, 1819–2005* (Singapore: NUS Press, 2009), p. 255.

74. "Free Trade, Say the Democrats," *The Straits Times*, 27 February 1955, p. 11. Yeo Kim Wah, for instance, comments in *Political Development in Singapore, 1945–1955* (Singapore: Singapore University Press, 1973) that the DP was founded to 'exploit Chinese communal feelings' (p. 134), and C. M. Turnbull mischaracterises the DP electoral pledges as one which aimed to 'foster Chinese education and culture, make Chinese an official language and obtain liberal citizenship terms for the China-born' (p. 255).

75. "Democrats are Still Shocked by Defeat," *The Straits Times*, 4 April 1955, p. 1.

76. "New Party Nothing to Do with Chamber," *The Singapore Free Press*, 22 February 1955, p. 1.

77. Visscher, *The Business of Politics and Ethnicity*, p. 109.

78. SCCC meeting minutes, 29 March 1956.

79. "Central Provident Fund to Pay More Interest—Lim," *The Straits Times*, 23 May 1957, p. 5.

80. "A Most Tragic Suggestion," *The Straits Times*, 27 April 1950, p. 9.

81. Singapore Legislative Assembly Debates, Third Session of the First Legislative Assembly, First Series, Vol 6, Part I of Session 1958, 23 April 1958, col 164.

82. Singapore Legislative Assembly Debates, Third Session of the First Legislative Assembly, First Series, Vol 7, Part II of Session 1958, 23 April 1958, col 164.

83. Comment by S. R. Nathan to Mr Tan Puay Hiang.

84. Sim Yau Tong's interview with the Oral History Centre (001312/2) discusses the various dialect groups in produce trade and the different sources/contacts, especially with Indians from Bombay.

85. "Training Malays in Chinese Firms," *The Straits Times*, 31 May 1956, p. 5.

86. Anecdote recounted by Mr Tan Puay Hiang.

87. "Chinese Syndicate Buys Cressonite," *The Straits Times*, 15 November 1951, p. 7.

88. *Nantah School News [南大校讯]*, Vol 1, No. 22, September 1969. However, only the Chinese versions have these sections; the English version is shorter and only discusses the landmark events of Nantah during the course of the year.

89. Wang Ruming, *These Fifty Years: Nantah's Fiftieth Anniversary, 1995–2005* (Singapore: Singapore Nantah Alumni, 2005) [王如明, *呵, 这五十年: 南洋大学创办五十周年纪念, 1955–2005* (新加坡: 新加坡南洋大学毕业生协会, 2005)], p. 29.

90. Quotes taken from Lee Guan Kin and Zhou Zhao Cheng, "The Split of the Ethnic Chinese and Their Separate Goals of Nation-Building," in *Demarcating Ethnicity in New Nations: Cases of the Chinese in Singapore, Malaysia, and Indonesia*, ed. Lee Guan Kin (Singapore: Singapore Society of Asian Studies, 2006), pp. 57–58.

91. *Ibid.*, p. 51.

92. Hu Xingrong, *Remebering Nantah* (Guilin: Guangxi Shifan University Press, 2006) [胡兴荣, *记忆南洋大学* (桂林: 广西师范大学出版社, 2006)], p. 13.

93. "Donations to Varsity," *The Straits Times*, 17 July 1950, p. 7.

94. Hu, *Remembering Nantah*, pp. 18–20.

95. "Members of University," *The Straits Times*, 22 August 1954, p. 9.

96. At this meeting, Tan Lark Sye announced that Nantah was not political, and that neither its student intake nor teaching medium were restricted to Chinese ["南洋大学绝无政治政治; 所收容的学生, 不限于华人; 而教授媒介, 也不限于华文华语"]. Hu, *Remembering Nantah* [胡兴荣, *记忆南洋大学*], p. 26.

97. "New Bid for Nanyang Compromise," *The Straits Times*, 22 February 1955, p. 1.

98. "Nanyang Row the Final Chapter," *The Straits Times*, 7 April 1955, p. 9.

99. Edwin Lee, *Singapore: The Unexpected Nation* (Singapore: Institute of Southeast Asian Studies, 2008), p. 421.

100. "Lark Sye Verdict: His Citizenship Revoked," *The Straits Times*, 18 July 1964, p. 1.

101. "Nantah Reshuffle 'Must' in Fight for Recognition," *The Straits Times*, 3 October 1963, p. 20.

102. Lim Beng Tee, "'Yes' by Nanyang," *The Straits Times*, 9 July 1964, p. 1.

103. "Nantah Always to Be the Chinese Varsity of S'pore, Says Govt," *The Straits Times*, 16 November 1965, p. 8.

104. "Nanyang: Chance to Rejoin for Students," *The Straits Times*, 20 November 1965, p. 4.

105. "When a Merchant Banker Turns Diplomat," *The Straits Times*, 1 May 1966, p. 8.

106. Song, *Biographies of Singapore-Malaya Personalities* [宋, 星马人物志], p. 61.

107. "Service Medal to Tan Siak Kew," *Singapore Trade and Industry*, July 1962, p. 36.

108. "Four to Get Honorary Awards," *The Straits Times*, 23 July 1974, p. 6.

109. "1957 — A Boom Year for Trade in Colony," *The Straits Times*, 26 January 1958, p. 9; "Singapore 'liberal trading' pledge," *The Straits Times*, 24 January 1958, p. 1.

110. Ho Rih Hwa, *Eating Salt: An Autobiography* (Singapore: Times Books International, 1991), pp. 256–257.

111. Gretchen Liu, *The Singapore Foreign Service: The First 40 Years* (Singapore: Editions Didier Millet, 2005), p. 65.

112. S.R. Nathan, with Timothy Auger, *An Unexpected Journey: Path to the Presidency* (Singapore: Editions Didier Millet, 2011), p. 427.

113. "Singapore Celebrates National Day," *Bangkok Post*, 9 August 1967.

114. Liu, *The Singapore Foreign Service*, p. 65.

115. Nathan, *An Unexpected Journey*, p. 296.

116. Ho, *Eating Salt*, p. 257.

117. "Director Known for Services to State," *The Straits Times*, 1 February 1964, p. 17.

118. Song, *Biographies of Singapore-Malaya Personalities*, p. 61

119. He was Vice-President in 1934 ("Siong Boo A.A.," *The Singapore Free Press and Mercantile Advertiser*, 4 May 1934, p. 15) and President in 1936

("Siong Boo Athletic Association Dinner," *The Singapore Free Press and Mercantile Advertiser*, 24 February 1936, p. 16). From 1938 onwards, he was patron of the Association ("Siong Boo A.A. Officers," *The Straits Times*, 15 May 1938, p. 31).

120. "Obituary," *The Straits Times*, 8 February 1977, p. 22 ; "Acknowledgements," *The Straits Times*, 15 February 1977, p. 35

121. *Ibid.*

122. "'Personal' Names for New Roads," *The Straits Times*, 27 September 1951, p. 7

123. "Director Known for Services to State," *The Straits Times*, 1 February 1964, p. 17

Acknowledgements

It is not your business to determine how good it is, nor how it compares with other expressions. It is your business to keep it yours clearly and directly, to keep the channel open... You have to keep yourself open and aware directly to the urges that motivate you... No artist is pleased. There is no satisfaction whatever at any time. There is only a queer divine dissatisfaction, a blessed unrest that keeps us marching and makes us more alive than the others.

— *Martha Graham (1894–1991)*

Writing a publication such as this is a difficult and trying process, especially for a greenhorn like myself. Heeding Martha Graham's call, it is not my business to determine how good my work is, but it is my business to give thanks to those who had channelled their support to this book — those helpful individuals who had blessed this blessed unrest.

First of all, I would like to extend my thanks to the Tan family — in particular Mr Tan Puay Hiang, the youngest son of

Tan Siak Kew — who entrusted an outsider to the family and a fresh graduate of the National University of Singapore's History Department to undertake such a mammoth task. This publication owes a tremendous debt to his selfless sharing of memories about his father and the offer of many photographs to visually enrich the text.

I am also grateful to Professor Lim Chong Yah, as without his generous sharing of his memories about Tan Siak Kew in Bangkok, the chapter on the latter's diplomatic life would have been significantly shorter. Mr S. R. Nathan's kind words and support for the project, succinctly placed in his foreword which graces this publication, is also much appreciated.

Along the way, many repositories of knowledge and their helpful staff have been crucial to the project. In addition to the wonderful and amazing collection on overseas Chinese at the National University of Singapore Central Library, the Lee Kong Chian reference collection at the National Library of Singapore and the records at the National Archives of Singapore (NAS) have been indispensable to the research.

Special thanks is also due to the Singapore Chinese Chamber of Commerce, with the prompt responses offered by Ms Tan Siew Kiang who so readily provided access to the meeting minutes deposited with NAS. Special mention must also be given to Ms Florence Lo, the tireless researcher who helped with the reading of these hand-written minutes on the glaring microfilm screens and transcribed it to the typed Chinese script which made it so much easier on my eyes.

Last but not least, I would like to thank World Scientific Publishing. This book was a result of Chief Editor Professor K. K. Phua's encouragement that Tan Siak Kew's public life was too significant to go unrecorded. In addition to the incisive and timely editorial provided by both Ms Chye Shu Wen and Ms Rajni Nayanthara

Gamage, this publication has also benefited immensely from the contacts shared by its first editor.

The process was not always divinely smooth-sailing, and I must squeeze in mention of — without listing — the many more friends and family members who have reminded me of Martha Graham's exhortation to take comfort in dissatisfaction. While I cannot assume responsibility for determining the worth of this book, I will take ownership of any errors contained it. May this blessed unrest keep us all marching forth in search of the pioneers of Singapore, who bravely went against the grain.

About the Author

F iona Tan is an independent scholar and researcher who gradu- ated from the National University of Singapore's History Department. Her research interests lie in colonial Malayan history, Singapore history, and micro-history. This is her first full-length publication.

Index

Printed in the United States
By Bookmasters